Chicago

A Musical Vaudeville

Book by Fred Ebb and Bob Fosse
Music by John Kander
Lyrics by Fred Ebb

Based on the play "Chicago"
by Maurine Dallas Watkins

A SAMUEL FRENCH ACTING EDITION

SAMUEL FRENCH

FOUNDED 1830

New York Hollywood London Toronto

SAMUELFRENCH.COM

RENTAL MATERIALS

An orchestration consisting of a Conductor/Rehearsal Piano Score, Reed 1 (piccolo, clarinet, soprano & alto saxophones), Reed 2 (piccolo, clarinet, bass clarinet, soprano & tenor saxophones) Reed 3 (clarinet, bass clarinet, soprano, tenor & baritone saxophones) Trumpets 1 & 2, Trombone 1, Trombone 2, Tuba/Bass, Percussion (glockenspiel, gong, drums) violin, Banjo, Keyboard 1 (piano, harmonium), Keyboard 2 (piano, accordion), and 20 Principal Chorus Books will be loaned two months prior to the production ONLY on the receipt of the Licensing Fee quoted for all performances, the rental fee and a refundable deposit.

Please contact Samuel French for perusal of the music materials as well as a performance license application.

ISBN   978-0-573-68081-6   Printed in U.S.A.   #126

ACT ONE

"ALL THAT JAZZ"—COPYRIGHT © 1973 AND 1975 BY KANDER-EBB, INC. AND UNICHAPPELL MUSIC, INC.

"FUNNY HONEY"—COPYRIGHT © 1973 AND 1975 BY KANDER-EBB, INC. AND UNICHAPPELL MUSIC, INC.

"CELL BLOCK TANGO"—COPYRIGHT © 1975 BY KANDER-EBB, INC. AND UNICHAPPELL MUSIC, INC.

"WHEN YOU'RE GOOD TO MAMA"—COPYRIGHT © 1975 BY KANDER-EBB, INC. AND UNICHAPPELL MUSIC, INC.

"TAP DANCE"—COPYRIGHT © 1973 AND 1975 BY KANDER-EBB, INC. AND UNICHAPPELL MUSIC, INC.

"ALL I CARE ABOUT"—COPYRIGHT © 1975 BY KANDER-EBB, INC. AND UNICHAPPELL MUSIC, INC.

"A LITTLE BIT OF GOOD"—COPYRIGHT © 1975 BY KANDER-EBB, INC. AND UNICHAPPELL MUSIC, INC.

"WE BOTH REACHED FOR THE GUN"—COPYRIGHT © 1975 BY KANDER-EBB, INC. AND UNICHAPPELL MUSIC, INC.

"ROXIE"—COPYRIGHT © 1974 AND 1975 BY KANDER-EBB, INC. AND UNICHAPPELL MUSIC, INC.

"I CAN'T DO IT ALONE"—COPYRIGHT © 1975 BY KANDER-EBB, INC. AND UNICHAPPELL MUSIC, INC.

"CHICAGO AFTER MIDNIGHT"—COPYRIGHT © 1973 AND 1975 BY KANDER-EBB, INC. AND UNICHAPPELL MUSIC, INC.

"MY OWN BEST FRIEND"—COPYRIGHT © 1973 AND 1975 BY KANDER-EBB, INC. AND UNICHAPPELL MUSIC, INC.

ACT TWO

"I KNOW A GIRL"—Copyright © 1973 and 1975 by Kander-Ebb, Inc. and Unichappell Music, Inc.

"ME AND MY BABY"—Copyright © 1974 and 1975 by Kander-Ebb, Inc. and Unichappell Music, Inc.

"MISTER CELLOPHANE"—Copyright © 1975 by Kander-Ebb, Inc. and Unichappell Music, Inc.

"WHEN VELMA TAKES THE STAND"—Copyright © 1975 by Kander-Ebb, Inc. and Unichappell Music, Inc.

"RAZZLE DAZZLE"—Copyright © 1974 and 1975 by Kander-Ebb, Inc. and Unichappell Music, Inc.

"CLASS"—Copyright © 1975 by Kander-Ebb, Inc. and Unichappell Music, Inc.

"NOWADAYS"—Copyright © 1975 by Kander-Ebb, Inc. and Unichappell Music, Inc.

*"R.S.V.P."—Copyright © 1975 by Kander-Ebb, Inc. and Unichappell Music, Inc.

*"KEEP IT HOT"—Copyright © 1975 by Kander-Ebb, Inc. and Unichappell Music, Inc.

* These two numbers will not be found in the musical material for the show, as they were deleted from the production and cannot be supplied.

FORTY-SIXTH STREET THEATRE

ROBERT FRYER and JAMES CRESSON

PRESENT

GWEN VERDON   CHITA RIVERA

AND

JERRY ORBACH

IN

A Musical Vaudeville

PRODUCED IN ASSOCIATION WITH
MARTIN RICHARDS
JOSEPH HARRIS and IRA BERNSTEIN

BOOK BY   MUSIC BY   LYRICS BY
FRED EBB and BOB FOSSE   JOHN KANDER   FRED EBB

BASED ON THE PLAY "CHICAGO" BY MAURINE DALLAS WATKINS

WITH
BARNEY MARTIN   MARY McCARTY   M. O'HAUGHEY

CANDY BROWN   CHRISTOPHER CHADMAN   CHERYL CLARK
GRACIELA DANIELE   GENE FOOTE   GARY GENDELL
RICHARD KORTHAZE   MICHON PEACOCK   CHARLENE RYAN
RON SCHWINN   PAUL SOLEN   PAMELA SOUSA
MICHAEL VITA

SETTINGS BY   COSTUMES BY   LIGHTING BY
TONY WALTON   PATRICIA ZIPPRODT   JULES FISHER

MUSICAL DIRECTOR   DANCE MUSIC ARRANGED BY
STANLEY LEBOWSKY   PETER HOWARD

ORCHESTRATIONS BY   SOUND DESIGN BY
RALPH BURNS   ABE JACOB

HAIR STYLES BY ROMAINE GREEN

DIRECTED AND CHOREOGRAPHED BY
BOB FOSSE

THE CAST
(in order of appearance)

VELMA KELLY .... *Chita Rivera*

ROXIE HART .... *Gwen Verdon*

FRED CASELY .... *Christopher Chadman*

SERGEANT FOGARTY .... *Richard Korthaze*

AMOS HART .... *Barney Martin*

LIZ .... *Cheryl Clark*

ANNIE .... *Michon Peacock*

JUNE .... *Candy Brown*

HUNYAK .... *Graciela Daniele*

MONA .... *Pamela Sousa*

MARTIN HARRISON .... *Michael Vita*

MATRON .... *Mary McCarty*

BILLY FLYNN .... *Jerry Orbach*

MARY SUNSHINE .... *M. O'Haughey*

GO-TO-HELL KITTY .... *Charlene Ryan*

HARRY .... *Paul Solen*

AARON .... *Gene Foote*

THE JUDGE .... *Ron Schwinn*

COURT CLERK .... *Gary Gendell*

THE SCENE

Chicago, Illinois. The late 1920's

MUSICAL NUMBERS

ACT ONE:

ALL THAT JAZZ .... *Velma and Company*
FUNNY HONEY .... *Roxie*
CELL BLOCK TANGO .... *Velma and the Girls*
WHEN YOU'RE GOOD TO MAMA .... *Matron*
TAP DANCE .... *Roxie, Amos and Boys*
ALL I CARE ABOUT .... *Billy and Girls*
A LITTLE BIT OF GOOD .... *Mary Sunshine*
WE BOTH REACHED FOR THE GUN .... *Billy, Roxie,*
Mary Sunshine and Company
ROXIE .... *Roxie and Boys*
I CAN'T DO IT ALONE .... *Velma*
CHICAGO AFTER MIDNIGHT .... *The Band*
MY OWN BEST FRIEND .... *Roxie and Velma*

ACT TWO:

I KNOW A GIRL .... *Velma*
ME AND MY BABY .... *Roxie and Boys*
MISTER CELLOPHANE .... *Amos*
WHEN VELMA TAKES THE STAND .. *Velma and Boys*
RAZZLE DAZZLE .... *Billy and Company*
CLASS .... *Velma and Matron*
NOWADAYS .... *Roxie*
NOWADAYS ⎫
R.S.V.P ⎬ .... *Roxie and Velma*
KEEP IT HOT ⎭

Chicago

ACT ONE

Scene 1

Scene: *Chicago, Illinois. The late '20's.*

At Rise: *Scrim Logo in.*

A Master of Ceremonies *enters and addresses the audience from in front of the scrim.*

Master of Ceremonies. Welcome. Ladies and gentlemen, you are about to see a story of murder, greed, corruption, violence, exploitation, adultery, and treachery—all those things we all hold near and dear to our hearts. Thank you. (*He walks off. A solo trumpet plays, the* Bandleader *counts off the overture. The Scrim rises. We see an on stage* Orchestra *on a platform suspended from a second level. They are seated above a Center Drum. The LIGHTS come up. The Doors of the Center Drum open, an elevator comes up and* Velma Kelly *enters. She walks forward to the audience. The Drum Doors close.*)

SONG: "ALL THAT JAZZ"

Velma. (*Sung.*)
COME ON, BABE
WHY DON'T WE PAINT THE TOWN?
AND ALL THAT JAZZ

I'M GONNA ROUGE MY KNEES
AND ROLL MY STOCKINGS DOWN
AND ALL THAT JAZZ

START THE CAR
I KNOW A WHOOPEE SPOT
WHERE THE GIN IS COLD
BUT THE PIANO'S HOT

9

IT'S JUST A NOISY HALL
WHERE THERE'S A NIGHTLY BRAWL
AND ALL THAT JAZZ!

(*The* COMPANY *enters.*)

SLICK YOUR HAIR
AND WEAR YOUR BUCKLE SHOES
AND ALL THAT JAZZ

I HEAR THAT FATHER DIP
IS GONNA BLOW THE BLUES
AND ALL THAT JAZZ

HOLD ON, HON
WE'RE GONNA BUNNY HUG
I BOUGHT SOME ASPIRIN
DOWN AT UNITED DRUG

IN CASE YOU SHAKE APART
AND WANT A BRAND NEW START
TO DO THAT –
   VELMA and COMPANY.
JAZZ.
   VELMA.
AND ALL THAT JAZZ

AND ALL THAT JAZZ
   COMPANY. (*Soft and diabolic.*)
HAH! HAH! HAH!

IT'S JUST A NOISY HALL
WHERE THERE'S A NIGHTLY BRAWL
AND ALL THAT JAZZ

   COMPANY. (*Single lines.*)
JAZZ!   (S. R. *Elevator comes up with* FRED CASELY
             and ROXIE HART. ROXIE *very drunk, hic-*
WHOOPEE!   *cups, and loses her shoe as she steps up*
             onto the stage. She grabs FRED *and pulls*
HOTCHA!   *him toward the Center Stage Drum Doors,*
             picking up her shoe on the way.)

FRED. (*Looking around.*) Listen, uh, your husband ain't home, is he? (ROXIE *shakes her head "No" as she "fishes" in her purse for the Door key.*)

VELMA. No, her husband is not at home. (*The Center Doors open and* ROXIE *goes into her apartment.* FRED *looks around and follows her. The Doors close.*)

VELMA. (*Sung.*)
FIND A FLASK
WE'RE PLAYING FAST AND LOOSE
   ALL.
AND ALL THAT JAZZ!

   VELMA.
RIGHT UP HERE
IS WHERE I STORE THE JUICE
   ALL.
AND ALL THAT JAZZ!

   VELMA.
COME ON, BABE
WE'RE GONNA BRUSH THE SKY
I BETCHA LUCKY LINDY
NEVER FLEW SO HIGH

'CAUSE IN THE STRATOSPHERE
HOW COULD HE LEND AN EAR
TO ALL THAT JAZZ?
   COMPANY.
OH, YOU'RE GONNA SEE YOUR SHEBA
SHIMMY SHAKE
   VELMA.
AND ALL THAT JAZZ
   COMPANY.
OH, SHE'S GONNA SHIMMY TILL HER GARTERS
   BREAK
   VELMA.
AND ALL THAT JAZZ
   COMPANY.
SHOW HER WHERE TO PARK HER GIRDLE
OH, HER MOTHER'S BLOOD'D CURDLE
IF SHE'D HEAR
HER BABY'S QUEER
FOR ALL THAT JAZZ!

(Music continues as the Drum Doors open. The Center Winch rolls in. We are in the HART bedroom. The bed is turned down. ROXIE is sprawled out on the bed in teddies.)

ROXIE. *(Calling.)* Oh, Fred . . . *(FRED appears. He takes off his pants. She holds the sheet back for him and he jumps into bed. The "Action" is very mechanical and business like. When it's over, FRED sits on the edge of the bed and pulls on his trousers. ROXIE sits up slowly—as if to say "Is that it?" FRED continues to get dressed as VELMA and the COMPANY sing.)*

VELMA.
AND ALL THAT JAZZ!

VELMA.	COMPANY.
COME ON, BABE	OH, YOU'RE GONNA SEE YOUR
WHY DON'T WE PAINT THE TOWN?	SHEBA
AND ALL THAT JAZZ	SHIMMY SHAKE
	AND ALL THAT JAZZ!
I'M GONNA	OH,
ROUGE MY KNEES	SHE'S GONNA SHIMMY
AND ROLL MY STOCKINGS DOWN	'TILL HER GARTERS BREAK
	AND ALL THAT JAZZ
START THE CAR	SHOW HER WHERE TO PARK HER
I KNOW A WHOOPEE SPOT	GIRDLE
WHERE THE GIN IS COLD	OH, HER MOTHER'S BLOOD'D
BUT THE PIANO'S HOT	CURDLE
IT'S JUST A NOISY HALL	IF SHE'D HEAR
WHERE THERE'S A NIGHTLY BRAWL	HER BABY'S QUEER
AND ALL THAT JAZZ!	FOR ALL THAT JAZZ!
	HOTCHA
	WHOOPEE
	JAZZ

(Music continues under.)

ROXIE. So that's final, huh Fred? *(FRED stands, puts on his jacket, and straightens his tie. ROXIE gets the gun from under the pillow.)*

FRED. Yeah, I'm afraid so, Roxie.

GIRLS. (*Calling.*) Oh, Fred . . .

FRED. (*Turning back to* ROXIE.) Yeah?

ROXIE. (*Pointing gun at him.*) *Nobody* walks out on me. (*She shoots him.*)

FRED. (*As he falls, clutching stomach.*) Sweetheart . . .

ROXIE. Don't "sweetheart" me, you son-of-a-bitch! (*She shoots him again. He dies. She drops the gun and looks bewildered—frightened—then nervously.*) Oh, I gotta pee. (ROXIE *runs off.*)

VELMA. (*Sung.*)
NO, I'M NO ONE'S WIFE
BUT, OH, I LOVE MY LIFE
AND ALL THAT JAZZ!

COMPANY.
THAT JAZZ!

BLACKOUT

SCENE 2

SCENE: *The bedroom. Three hours later.*

AT RISE: AMOS HART *is seated on the bed.* SERGEANT FOGARTY *is standing over him.* FOGARTY *is writing on a clipboard.*

AMOS. So I ah . . . took the gun, Officer, and I shot him.

FOGARTY. (*Writing.*) I see, and your wife, Roxie Hart, was in no way involved. Is that right?

AMOS. That's right, Officer. That's right.

FOGARTY. (*Finishing writing.*) Well . . . that's just fine. Sign right there, Mr. Hart.

AMOS. Freely and gladly. Freely and gladly.

FOGARTY. Oh, aren't you the cheerful little murderer, though?

AMOS. Murder? (*Correcting him.*) That's not murder, shootin' a burglar. Why just last week, the jury thanked a man. I say, thanked him.

FOGARTY. I guess you know your Chicago all right. Sign!

AMOS. (*Hesitantly.*) Yeah, freely and gladly. I say, freely and gladly. (AMOS *takes his fountain pen out of his pocket and nervously signs the confession.* FOGARTY *exits to check the other room. A Piano comes in on the* S. R. *Winch with* ROXIE *sitting on top of it, à la Helen Morgan. All during the following number, she drinks from a flask.)*

BANDLEADER. *(From the Bandstand.)* For her first number, Miss Roxie Hart would like to sing a song of love and devotion dedicated to her dear husband Amos. *(Music under.* AMOS *stares at* FRED CASELY'S *body lying on the floor in the middle of the room.)*

SONG: "FUNNY HONEY"

ROXIE. *(Sung.)*
SOMETIMES I'M RIGHT
SOMETIMES I'M WRONG
BUT HE DOESN'T CARE
HE'LL STRING ALONG
HE LOVES ME SO
THAT FUNNY HONEY OF MINE!

SOMETIMES I'M DOWN
SOMETIMES I'M UP
BUT HE FOLLOWS 'ROUND
LIKE SOME DROOPY-EYED PUP
HE LOVES ME SO
THAT FUNNY HONEY OF MINE

HE AIN'T NO SHEIK
THAT'S NO GREAT PHYSIQUE
LORD KNOWS, HE AIN'T GOT THE SMARTS

BUT LOOK AT THAT SOUL
I TELL YOU, THAT WHOLE
IS A WHOLE LOT GREATER
THAN THE SUM OF HIS PARTS

AND IF YOU KNEW HIM LIKE ME
I KNOW YOU'D AGREE

WHAT IF THE WORLD
SLANDERED MY NAME?
WHY, HE'D BE RIGHT THERE
TAKING THE BLAME

HE LOVES ME SO
AND IT ALL SUITS ME FINE
THAT FUNNY, SUNNY, HONEY
HUBBY OF MINE!

(FOGARTY *re-enters. Music continues under.*)

AMOS. (*To* FOGARTY.) A man got a right to protect his home and his loved ones, right?

FOGARTY. Of course, he has.

AMOS. (*Acting it out.*) Well, I come in from the garage, Officer, and I see him coming through the window.

FOGARTY. Uh-huh.

AMOS. With my wife Roxie there, sleepin' . . .

FOGARTY. Uh-huh.

AMOS. Like an angel . . . an angel!

ROXIE. (*Sung.*)
HE LOVES ME SO
THAT FUNNY HONEY OF MINE!

AMOS. I mean supposin', just supposin', he had violated her or somethin' . . . you know what I mean . . . violated?

FOGARTY. I know what you mean . . .

AMOS. . . . or somethin'. Think how terrible that would have been. Good thing I got home from work on time, I'm tellin' ya that! (FOGARTY *exits into other room.* AMOS *calls after him:*) I say I'm tellin' ya that!

ROXIE. (*Sung.*)
HE LOVES ME SO
THAT FUNNY HONEY OF MINE!

(FOGARTY *re-enters and begins examining the personal effects on the body.*)

FOGARTY. (*Looking in the wallet.*) Fred Casely.

AMOS. Fred Casely. *How could he be a burglar? My wife knows him! He sold us our furniture!*

ROXIE. (*Sung.*)
LORD KNOWS
HE AIN'T GOT THE SMARTS

AMOS. She lied to me. She told me he was a burglar.

FOGARTY. You mean he was dead when you got home?

Amos. She had him covered with a sheet and she's tellin' me that cock and bull story about this burglar, and I ought to say *I* did it 'cause I was sure to get off. *Burglar, huh!*

Roxie. (*Sung.*)
NOW, HE SHOT OFF
   HIS TRAP
I CAN'T STAND THAT
   SAP

LOOK AT HIM GO
RATTIN' ON ME
WITH JUST ONE MORE
   BRAIN
WHAT A HALF-WIT
   HE'D BE

IF THEY STRING ME
   UP
I'LL KNOW WHO
   BROUGHT THE
   TWINE

Amos. (*Under.*) And I believed her! That cheap little tramp. So, she was two-timin' me, huh? Well, then, she can swing for all I care. Boy, I'm down at the garage, working my butt off 14 hours a day, and she's up here muchin' on God-damn bon-bons and jazzing. This time she pushed me too far. That little chiseler. Boy, what a sap I was!

(Two Policemen *enter with a stretcher, they put* Casely *on it and exit.*)

THAT SCUMMY,
   CRUMMY
DUMMY HUBBY OF
   MINE

(*The number ends and* Roxie *slides off the piano and walks straight into the scene.*)

Roxie. You double crosser! You big blabber mouth. You said you'd stick! You promised you'd stick. How could you do this to me, your wife?

Amos. Ya been stringin' me, Roxanne. You told me he was a burglar and all the while you're up here jazzing him.

Roxie. (*Crossing to the bed.*) God damn you! You are a disloyal husband. (*To* FOGARTY.) I shot him. Put that down in your book.

AMOS. That's right. She shot him. I didn't have anything to do with it, Officer.

FOGARTY. Ah, now, we're getting to the real story.

ROXIE. And you wanna know why? He was tryin' to walk out on me. The louse.

FOGARTY. That's a pretty cold blooded murder, Mrs. Hart. They're liable to hang you for that one.

ROXIE. Hang me?

FOGARTY. (*With a laugh.*) Not so tough anymore, are you?

ROXIE. Amos, did you hear what he said? (AMOS *exits.*) Son-of-a-bitch . . . (*She quickly reaches into an open bureau drawer by the side of the bed, and pulls out a rosary.*) Hail Mary full of grace . . . (*LIGHTS DIM OUT, come up immediately on a* MASTER OF CEREMONIES S. L.)

MASTER OF CEREMONIES. And now, the six merry murderesses of the Cook County jail in their rendition of the Cell Block Tango.

SCENE 3

SCENE: *Limbo.*

AT RISE: *We see* VELMA *and five other* WOMEN PRISONERS *behind bars. Music under throughout.*

SONG: "CELL BLOCK TANGO"

FIRST GIRL. (LIZ.)
POP.

SECOND GIRL. (ANNIE.)
SIX.

THIRD GIRL. (JUNE.)
SQUISH.

FOURTH GIRL. (HUNYAK.)
UH UH.

FIFTH GIRL. (VELMA.)
CICERO.

SIXTH GIRL. (MONA.)
LIPSCHITZ!

(*Percussion under.*)

LIZ.
POP
ANNIE.
SIX
JUNE.
SQUISH
HUNYAK.
UH UH
VELMA.
CICERO
MONA.
LIPSCHITZ!

(*Now the rhythm is steady and insistent.*)

LIZ.
POP
ANNIE.
SIX
JUNE.
SQUISH
HUNYAK.
UH UH
VELMA.
CICERO
MONA.
LIPSCHITZ
LIZ.
POP
ANNIE.
SIX
JUNE.
SQUISH
HUNYAK.
UH UH
VELMA.
CICERO
MONA.
LIPSCHITZ!

ALL.
HE HAD IT COMING
HE HAD IT COMING
HE ONLY HAD HIMSELF TO BLAME
IF YOU'D HAVE BEEN THERE
IF YOU'D HAVE SEEN IT
VELMA.
I BETCHA YOU WOULD HAVE DONE THE SAME!
LIZ.
POP
ANNIE.
SIX
JUNE.
SQUISH
HUNYAK.
UH UH
VELMA.
CICERO
MONA.
LIPSCHITZ!

LIZ. You know how people have these little habits that get you down. Like Bernie. Bernie liked to chew gum. No, not chew. POP. Well, I came home this one day and I am really irritated, and looking for a little sympathy and there's Bernie layin' on the couch, drinkin' a beer and chewin'. No, not chewin'. Poppin'. So I said to him, I said, "Bernie, you pop that gum one more time . . . " and he did. So I took the shotgun off the wall and I fired two warning shots . . . into his head.

GIRLS. (*Under.*)
HE HAD IT COMING
HE HAD IT COMING
HE ONLY HAD HIM-
SELF TO BLAME
IF YOU'D HAVE BEEN
THERE
IF YOU'D HAVE SEEN
IT
I BETCHA YOU WOULD
HAVE DONE THE
SAME
HE HAD IT COMING
HE HAD IT COMING
HE ONLY HAD HIM-
SELF TO BLAME
IF YOU'D HAVE BEEN
THERE
IF YOU'D HAVE SEEN
IT
(*Continue to cue.*)

ALL.
HE HAD IT COMING
HE HAD IT COMING
HE ONLY HAD HIMSELF TO BLAME

ANNIE. I met Ezekial Young from Salt Lake City about two years ago and he told me he was single and we hit it off right away. So, we started living together. He'd go to work, he'd come home, I'd mix him a drink, we'd have dinner. Well, it was like heaven in two and a half rooms. And then I found out, "Single" he told me? Single, my ass. Not only was he married . . . oh, no, he had six wives. One of those Mormons, you know. So that night, when he came home, I mixed him his drink, as usual. You know, some guys just can't hold their arsenic.

GIRLS. (*Under.*)
IF YOU'D HAVE BEEN THERE
IF YOU'D HAVE HEARD IT
I BETCHA YOU WOULD HAVE DONE THE SAME!

HE HAD IT COMING
HE HAD IT COMING
HE ONLY HAD HIMSELF TO BLAME
(*Continue to cue.*)

LIZ, ANNIE, JUNE, MONA.
HE HAD IT COMING

HE HAD IT COMING
HE TOOK A FLOWER
   IN ITS PRIME
AND THEN HE USED
   IT
AND HE ABUSED IT
IT WAS A MURDER
   BUT NOT A CRIME!

VELMA and HUNYAK.
POP, SIX, SQUISH, UH UH,
CICERO, LIPSCHITZ

POP, SIX, SQUISH, UH UH,
CICERO, LIPSCHITZ

POP, SIX, SQUISH, UH UH,
CICERO, LIPSCHITZ
GIRLS. (*Under.*)

JUNE. (*Matter of factly.*)
Now, I'm standing in the
POP, SIX, UH UH,

kitchen carvin' up the chicken for dinner, minding my own

CICERO,

LIPSCHITZ

business, and in storms my husband Wilbur, in a jealous rage. "You been screwin' the milkman," he says. He was crazy and he kept screamin', "You been screwin' the milkman." And then he ran into my knife. He ran into my knife ten times.

POP, SIX, UH UH,
   CICERO,
LIPSCHITZ

POP, SIX, UH UH,
   CICERO,
LIPSCHITZ

ALL.

IF YOU'D HAVE BEEN THERE
IF YOU'D HAVE SEEN IT
I BETCHA YOU WOULD HAVE DONE THE SAME!

HUNYAK. Mit keresek, én itt? Azt mondjok, hogy a hires lakem lefogta a férjemet en meg lecsaptam a fejét. De nem igaz, en ártatlan vagyok. Nem tudom mert mondja Uncle Sam hõgy en tettem. Probáltam a rendorsegén megmagyarazni de nem ertettek meg . . .

JUNE. But did you *do* it?

HUNYAK. UH UH, not guilty!

VELMA. My sister, Veronica, and I did this double act and my husband, Charlie, traveled around with us. Now, for the last number in our act, we did these 20 acrobatic tricks in a row, one, two, three, four, five, . . . splits, spread eagles, flip flops, back flips, one right after the other. Well, this one night we were in Cicero, the three of us, sittin' up in a hotel room, boozin' and havin' a few laughs and we ran out of ice, so I went out to get some. I come back, open the door and there's Veronica and Charlie doing number Seven-

GIRLS. (*Under.*)

HE HAD IT COMING
HE HAD IT COMING
HE ONLY HAD HIM-
   SELF TO BLAME
IF YOU'D HAVE BEEN
   THERE
IF YOU'D HAVE SEEN·
   IT

I BETCHA YOU WOULD
   HAVE DONE THE
   SAME!
HE HAD IT COMING
HE HAD IT COMING
HE TOOK A FLOWER IN
   ITS PRIME
THEN HE USED IT . . .

teen—the spread eagle. Well, I was in such a state of shock, I completely blacked out. I can't remember a thing. It wasn't until later, when I was washing the blood off my hands I even knew they were dead. (*Sung.*)

THEY HAD IT COMING
THEY HAD IT COMING
THEY HAD IT COMING ALL ALONG
I DIDN'T DO IT
BUT IF I'D DONE IT
HOW COULD YOU TELL ME THAT I WAS WRONG?

VELMA.

THEY HAD IT COMING
THEY HAD IT COMING
THEY HAD IT COMING
  ALL ALONG
I DIDN'T DO IT
BUT IF I'D DONE IT
HOW COULD YOU TELL
  ME THAT
I WAS WRONG?

GIRLS. (*Under.*)

THEY HAD IT COMING
THEY HAD IT COMING
THEY TOOK A FLOWER
  IN IT'S PRIME
AND THEN THEY USED
  IT
AND THEY ABUSED IT
IT WAS A MURDER,
  BUT NOT A CRIME!

GIRLS. (*Under.*)

HE HAD IT COMING
HE HAD IT COMING
HE ONLY HAD HIM-
  SELF TO BLAME
IF YOU'D HAVE BEEN
  THERE
IF YOU'D HAVE SEEN
  IT

I BETCHA YOU WOULD
HAVE DONE THE
SAME.

MONA. I loved Alvin Lipschitz more than I can possibly say. He was a real artistic guy . . . sensitive . . . a painter. But he was troubled. He was always trying to find himself. He'd go out every night looking for himself and on the way he found Ruth, Gladys, Rosemary and Irving. I guess you can say we broke up because of artistic differences. He saw himself as alive and I saw him dead.

ALL.

THE DIRTY BUM, BUM, BUM

THE DIRTY BUM, BUM, BUM (*Etc.*) CONTINUE . . .

Liz, Annie, Mona.	Velma and June.	Hunyak.
THEY HAD IT COMIN'	(*Answer chorus.*)	(*Ad-lib.*)
THEY HAD IT COMIN'	THEY HAD IT COMIN'	
THEY HAD IT COMIN'	THEY HAD IT COMIN'	
ALL ALONG	THEY HAD IT COMIN'	
	ALL ALONG	
'CAUSE IF THEY USED US		
AND THEY ABUSED US	'CAUSE IF THEY USED US	
HOW COULD YOU TELL US	AND THEY ABUSED US	
THAT WE WERE WRONG?	HOW COULD YOU TELL US	
	THAT WE WERE WRONG?	

All.
HE HAD IT COMING
HE HAD IT COMING
HE ONLY HAD HIMSELF
TO BLAME
IF YOU'D HAVE BEEN THERE
IF YOU'D HAVE SEEN IT
I BETCHA YOU WOULD HAVE DONE THE SAME

(*They back into the Center Drum.*)

Liz. You pop that gum one more time!
Annie. Single my ass.
June. Ten times!
Hunyak. Miért csukott Uncle Sam bortonbe.
Velma. Number Seventeen—the spread eagle.
Mona. Artistic differences.
All. (*Sung.*)
I BETCHA YOU WOULD HAVE DONE THE SAME!

BLACKOUT

SCENE 4

SCENE: *Limbo.*

AT RISE: MASTER OF CEREMONIES *enters from* S. R., *brings a microphone Center Stage.*

MASTER OF CEREMONIES. And now, ladies and gentlemen— the Keeper of the Keys, the Countess of the Clink, the Mistress of Murderer's row—Matron Mama Morton! (MATRON MORTON *enters. She is wearing a large ring, a fur stole with a large orchid corsage, and has a large handkerchief tied to the ring á la Sophie Tucker. The* MASTER OF CEREMONIES *removes the* MATRON'S *stole from her shoulders and exits.*)

SONG: "WHEN YOU'RE GOOD TO MAMA"

MATRON. (*Sung.*)
ASK ANY OF THE CHICKIES IN MY PEN
THEY'LL TELL YOU I'M THE BIGGEST MOTHER
    HEN
I LOVE THEM ALL AND ALL OF THEM LOVE ME
BECAUSE THE SYSTEM WORKS
THE SYSTEM CALLED RECIPROCITY . . .

GOT A LITTLE MOTTO
ALWAYS SEES ME THROUGH
WHEN YOU'RE GOOD TO MAMA
MAMA'S GOOD TO YOU

THERE'S A LOT OF FAVORS
I'M PREPARED TO DO
YOU DO ONE FOR MAMA
SHE'LL DO ONE FOR YOU.

THEY SAY THAT LIFE IS TIT FOR TAT
AND THAT'S THE WAY I LIVE
SO, I DESERVE A LOT OF TAT
FOR WHAT I'VE GOT TO GIVE

DON'T YOU KNOW THAT THIS HAND
WASHES THAT ONE TOO

WHEN YOU'RE GOOD TO MAMA
MAMA'S GOOD TO YOU!

(VELMA *rides in on* S. L. *Winch. There are many newspapers on the table in front of her.* MATRON *crosses to her.* VELMA *holds up a paper.*)

VELMA. Look at this, Mama. The Tribune calls me the crime of the year. (*Holds up another paper.*) And the News says . . . (*Reading from the paper.*) "Not in memory do we recall so fiendish and horrible a double homicide."

MATRON. Ah, Baby, you couldn't buy that kind of publicity. You took care of Mama and Mama took care of you. I talked to Flynn. He set your trial date for March the 5th. March 7th you'll be acquitted. And March 8th—do you know what Mama's gonna do for you?— She's gonna start you on a vaudeville tour.

VELMA. I been on a lot of vaudeville tours, Mama. What kind of dough are we talking about?

MATRON. It's a crazy world, kid. Babe Ruth, the baseball player, is wearing lipstick and rouge and playing the Palace making five thousand a week.

VELMA. (*Interrupting.*) I said what kind of dough are *we* talking about, Mama?

MATRON. Well, I been talkin' to the boys at William Morris and due to your recent sensational activities I can get you twenty-five hundred.

VELMA. (*Flabbergasted.*) Twenty-five hundred! The most me and Veronica ever made *together* was three-fifty.

MATRON. That was before Cicero, before Billy Flynn, and *before Mama.*

VELMA. Mama, I always wanted to play Big Jim Colisimo's. Could you get me that?

MATRON. Big Jim's! Well now, that's another story. That might take another phone call.

VELMA. (*Nods, knowingly.*) Uh, uh. And how much would *that* phone call cost?

MATRON. Come on, Vel, you know how I feel about you. You're my favorite. You're the classiest dame in this whole joint. You're like family to me—like my own. I'll do it for 50 bucks.

VELMA. (*Resigned, hands her the money.*) Fifty bucks for a phone call. (MATRON *steps off winch, walks Center. Winch starts to ride* VELMA *off stage.*) You must get a lot of wrong numbers, Mama. (*Winch off.*)

MATRON. (*Sung.*)
IF YOU WANT MY GRAVY
PEPPER MY RAGOUT
SPICE IT UP FOR MAMA
SHE'LL GET HOT FOR YOU

WHEN THEY PASS THAT BASKET
FOLKS CONTRIBUTE TO
YOU PUT IN FOR MAMA
SHE'LL PUT OUT FOR YOU

THE FOLKS ATOP THE LADDER
ARE THE ONES THE WORLD ADORES
SO BOOST ME UP MY LADDER, KID
AND I'LL BOOST YOU UP YOURS

LET'S ALL STROKE TOGETHER
LIKE THE PRINCETON CREW
WHEN YOU'RE STROKIN' MAMA
MAMA'S STROKIN' YOU

SO WHAT'S THE ONE CONCLUSION
I CAN BRING THIS NUMBER TO?

WHEN YOU'RE GOOD TO MAMA
MAMA'S GOOD TO YOU!

BLACKOUT

SCENE 5

SCENE: *The Jail.*

AT RISE: *Drum Doors open. Center Winch rolls out with jail set. The* MATRON *walks back into scene, sits at table, and starts to knit.* ROXIE *hangs onto the jail bars with her back to the audience. We hear a clarinet solo from the Bandstand.* KATALIN HUNYAK *sits in a cell, Stage Right, looking at the floor.* MUNA *is seated in a cell Stage Left sculpting a clay figurine.* JUNE *enters from the Stage Left stairs.*

JUNE. (*To the* MATRON.) Mrs. Morton, if my husband, Wilbur, comes here to visit me, you tell him I do not want to see him.

MATRON. June, your husband is dead, you killed him.

JUNE. Oh well, forget it then. (JUNE *exits back up the stairs.* VELMA *comes up the stairs from the pit.*)

VELMA. (*To* ROXIE.) Hey you! Red! Get out of my chair!

ROXIE. Who the hell . . .

MATRON. (*Warningly.*) Roxie, Roxie, this here is Velma Kelly.

ROXIE. Velma Kelly? THE Velma Kelly? Oh, gosh, I sure am pleased to meet you. I read about you in the papers all the time. (*To the* MATRON.) I love to follow the murders. (*To* VELMA.) Yours is my favorite.

VELMA. (*The Duchess.*) Thanks, kid.

ROXIE. Miss Kelly, could I ask you somethin'?

VELMA. (*Suspiciously.*) What?

ROXIE. The Assistant District Attorney, Mr. Harrison, said what I done was a hanging case and he's prepared to ask the maximum penalty.

VELMA. Yeah, so?

ROXIE. So, I'm scared. I sure would appreciate some advice . . .

VELMA. (*To* ROXIE.) Look, I don't give no advice. I don't get any and I don't give any. You're a perfect stranger to me and let's keep it that way, okay? And that's the way it is around here.

ROXIE. (*With some bitterness.*) Thanks for the help.

VELMA. You're welcome.

MATRON. Well, I'd like to help you, dearie. (ANNIE *enters, goes to* MATRON MORTON *and taps her on the shoulder.* MATRON *notices* ANNIE.) Gin or bourbon?

ANNIE. Bourbon. (ANNIE *hands money to the* MATRON. *The* MATRON *gives her change as she continues talking.* ANNIE *exits.*)

MATRON. (*To* ROXIE.) First, what do you figure on using for grounds? What are you gonna tell the Jury?

ROXIE. I guess . . . I'll just tell them the truth.

MATRON. Are you crazy! You can't tell 'em that, dearie.

VELMA. (*Laughing.*) Tellin' a jury the truth, that's really stupid.

MATRON. You see, dearie, it's this way. Murder is like divorce. The reason don't count. It's the grounds. Temporary insanity . . . self-defense . . .

ROXIE. (*To* VELMA.) Yeah, what's your grounds?

VELMA. My grounds are that I didn't do it.

ROXIE. So, who did?

VELMA. Well, I'm sure I don't know. I passed out completely. I can't remember a thing. Only I'm sure I didn't do it. I've the tenderest heart in the world. Haven't I, Mama?

MATRON. You bet your ass you have, Velma.

ROXIE. Is being drunk grounds?

VELMA. Just ask your lawyer.

ROXIE. I ain't got a lawyer.

VELMA. Well, as they say in Southampton . . . you are shit out of luck, my dear.

ROXIE. (*Panicked,* ROXIE *pulls out her rosary and sinks to her knees.*) Hail Mary, full of grace, the Lord is with thee . . . Blessed art Thou amongst women. Blessed is the fruit of thy womb. (MATRON *takes the beads away from* ROXIE.)

MATRON. (*Interrupting.*) Roxie, relax, relax. In this town, murder is a form of entertainment. Besides, in forty-seven years, Cook County ain't never hung a woman yet. So it's forty-seven to one, they won't hang you.

VELMA. There's always a first time.

MATRON. Ah, Vel. A conviction, maybe.

ROXIE. Conviction, maybe?

VELMA. Yeah, that's right.

ROXIE. What's that?

VELMA. Life.

ROXIE. In jail?

VELMA. Where else? Marshall Field?

ROXIE. (*Grabs beads, starts to play again.*) Oh, Jesus, Mary and Joseph.

VELMA. (*Jumping up.*) Boy, you know everybody.

MATRON. Velma, lay off of her.

VELMA. What do I give a damn about her? (*Starts off.*)

Enough of these trashy religious fanatics. I think I shall retire to my cell and take a wee nap and answer some fan mail. Would you wake me when luncheon is served, Mama? (*She exits down the pit stairs.*)

MATRON. My pleasure, Velma.

ROXIE. So that's Velma Kelly.

MATRON. Yeah.

ROXIE. She sure don't look like a Kelly to me.

MATRON. Oh, Kelly's her stage name. That Velma's really somethin'. She wears nothing but Black Narcissus Perfume and never makes her own bed.

ROXIE. I thought you had to.

MATRON. No, I take care of that for her.

ROXIE. You make her bed?

MATRON. Well, not exactly. You see, Velma pays me five dollars a week, then I give the Hungarian fifty cents and she does it. She needs the money, poor thing. Hey, Katalin Hunyak, szeretnem ha megismerned Roxie Hart ot.

HUNYAK. (*From her cell.*) Not guilty.

MATRON. That's all she ever says. Anyway, Velma has her laundry sent out and that cost five dollars more. She has her meals sent in from Wooster's Drug Store around the corner. That costs her twenty. And you know who's defending her, don't ya?

ROXIE. No. Who's defending her?

MATRON. Mr. Billy Flynn! Best criminal lawyer in all Chicago, that's all. (*Laughs.*) What he don't know about juries and women!

ROXIE. How do you get Billy Flynn?

MATRON. Not by praying, dearie. First you give me a hundred dollars, then I make a phone call.

ROXIE. I see, and how much does he get?

MATRON. Five thousand dollars.

ROXIE. Five thousand dollars!

MATRON. Well, he's worth every cent. Never lost a case for a female client yet.

ROXIE. Never?

MATRON. Never! (*The* MATRON *puts her hand on* ROXIE's *knee.*) I'd be happy to make that phone call for you, dearie.

ROXIE. Thanks for fillin' me in. We'll talk later, okay? (ROXIE *rises and steps off the platform.*)

MATRON. You bet we will. (*Lights fade on the jail as the Center Winch moves back.* ROXIE *walks to the edge of* S. R. *She sits on the edge of the stage level, with her feet on the* S. R. *elevator. The elevator goes down as she stands, until we only see her from the waist up. Lights up on Visitors' Area. Drum Doors close.*)

ROXIE. Five thousand dollars! Now, where in hell am I gonna get five thousand dollars?!

SCENE 6

SCENE: *The Visitors' Area.*

AT RISE: *A* MASTER OF CEREMONIES *enters and sets up a wire cage Down Stage Center to create the effect of a Visitors' Area for the next scene.*

MASTER OF CEREMONIES. (*From Center Stage.*) Ladies and gentlemen, a tap dance. (MASTER OF CEREMONIES *exits.* AMOS *appears on the other side of the wire cage. We can only see him from the waist up, too.* ROXIE *walks to* AMOS, *talks to him through the wire.* FOUR MEN *enter on stage level and dance* ["TAP DANCE"] *throughout the following Scene.*)

ROXIE. (*To* AMOS *with great feeling.*) Oh, Amos, I knew you'd come. Amos, I know I've been sinful, but I'm changin'. All I want now is to make up to you for what I done. And I will, Amos, just as soon as I get out of here. And I *can* get out of here, too. You see, there's this lawyer, and he costs five thousand dollars. (AMOS *drops the cigar out of his mouth.*)

AMOS. Roxie, I'm tired of your fancy foot work. The answer is "no."

ROXIE. Oh Amos, I know I lied to you. I know I've cheated on you with other men. Oh Amos, I've even stolen money from your pants pockets while you were sleepin'.

AMOS. You did?

ROXIE. But I never stopped loving you, not ever—and I always thought—my Amos, he's so manly and so attractive and so . . . I'm embarrassed . . . so sexy.

AMOS. Honest?

ROXIE. Honest.

AMOS. But, five thousand bucks . . .

Roxie. It's my hour of need for chrissakes!

Amos. Well, okay. I'll get it for you, Roxie. I'll get it. (Four Men *finish the dance.* Roxie *nods a bow to the audience.*)

BLACKOUT

Scene 7

Scene: *Limbo.*

At Rise: *Lights come up on a* Master of Ceremonies *Stage Right.*

Master of Ceremonies. Ladies and gentlemen, presenting the Silver Tongued Prince of the Courtroom—the one—the only Mr. Billy Flynn. (*Lights come up on* Six Girls *posed in the show logo Center Stage.*)

SONG: "ALL I CARE ABOUT"

Girls. (*Sung.*)
WE WANT BILLY
WHERE IS BILLY?
GIVE US BILLY
WE WANT BILLY
B. I. DOUBLE L. Y.
WE'RE ALL HIS
HE'S OUR KIND OF A GUY
AND OOH WHAT LUCK
'CAUSE HERE HE IS.

(*Center Drum Doors partially open.* Billy Flynn *appears in silhouette. He is dressed "to the teeth," and very elegant. During the following Fan Dance with the* Girls, *he strips to his underwear.*)

Billy. (*Spoken—a la Ted Lewis.*) Is everybody here? Is everybody ready? (*Walks down to audience. Center Drum Doors close. Sung:*)
I DON'T CARE ABOUT EXPENSIVE THINGS

CASHMERE COATS, DIAMOND RINGS
DON'T MEAN A THING
ALL I CARE ABOUT IS LOVE
  GIRLS.
THAT'S WHAT HE'S HERE FOR
  BILLY.
I DON'T CARE FOR WEARIN' SILK CRAVATS
RUBY STUDS, SATIN SPATS
DON'T MEAN A THING
ALL I CARE ABOUT IS LOVE
  GIRLS.
ALL HE CARES ABOUT IS LOVE
  BILLY.
GIMME TWO EYES OF BLUE
SOFTLY SAYING, "I NEED YOU"
LET ME SEE HER STANDIN' THERE
AND HONEST MISTER, I'M A MILLIONAIRE

I DON'T CARE FOR ANY FINE ATTIRE
VANDERBILT MIGHT ADMIRE
NO, NO, NOT ME
ALL I CARE ABOUT IS LOVE . . .
  GIRLS.
ALL HE CARES ABOUT IS LOVE.

(GIRLS *hum* . . . BILLY *addresses the audience.*)

BILLY. (*Spoken.*) Maybe you think I'm talking about *physical* love. Well, I'm not. Not *just* physical love. There's other kinds of love. Like love of . . . justice. Love of . . . legal procedure. Love of lending a hand to someone who really needs you. Love of your fellow man. *Those* kinds of love are what I'm talkin' about. And physical love ain't so bad either. (*Back into song. Whistle chorus too. Sung.*)
IT MAY SOUND ODD
BUT ALL I CARE ABOUT IS LOVE
  GIRLS.
THAT'S WHAT HE'S HERE FOR
  BILLY. (*Boo Boo Chorus to:*)
HONEST TO GOD

ALL I CARE ABOUT IS LOVE
  GIRLS.
ALL HE CARES ABOUT IS LOVE
  BILLY.
SHOW ME LONG, LONG RAVEN HAIR
FLOWIN' DOWN, ABOUT TO THERE
AND WHEN I SEE HER RUNNIN' FREE
KEEP YOUR MONEY, THAT'S ENOUGH FOR ME

(GIRLS "Ah.")

I DON'T CARE FOR DRIVIN' PACKARD CARS
OR SMOKING LONG, BUCK CIGARS
NO, NO, NOT ME
ALL I CARE ABOUT IS
DOIN' THE GUY IN
WHO'S PICKIN' ON YOU
TWISTIN' THE WRIST
THAT'S TURNIN' THE SCREW
  ALL.
ALL I (HE) CARE(S) ABOUT IS LOVE!

(*The* GIRLS *dance off.* BILLY, *in his underwear, walks back into the following scene.*)

SCENE 8

SCENE: BILLY'S *office.*

AT RISE: *Drum Doors open. Center Winch, now* BILLY'S *office, rolls down.* AMOS *is seated in front of* BILLY'S *desk.* BILLY *puts on the trousers of a suit that is obviously being made for him. A* TAILOR, *on his knees, his mouth full of pins, measures* BILLY. *During the following dialogue, the* TAILOR *continues to measure him.*

  BILLY. (*To* AMOS.) Well, hello, Andy.
  AMOS. Amos. My name is Amos.

BILLY. Right. Did you bring the rest of the five thousand dollars?

AMOS. I . . . I didn't do as well as I hoped. (*Puts up a restraining hand.*) But I will, Mr. Flynn. I will, all right. (*Takes certificates, books, etc. from pocket.*) Here's five hundred on my insurance.

BILLY. That makes a thousand. (*To the* TAILOR, *who has stuck him with a pin.*) Ow! Ya dumb fruit!

TAILOR. Oh, I *am* sorry, Mr. Flynn.

AMOS. And three hundred dollars that I borrowed from the guys at the garage. (*Puts it on the desk.*) . . . and seven hundred out of the building and loan fund . . .

BILLY. That's two thousand.

AMOS. And that's all I got so far.

BILLY. What about her father?

AMOS. Oh yeah, her father . . . I phoned him yesterday . . . long distance . . . and he said . . . well, he told me he'll probably be able to raise some money later.

BILLY. You're a damned liar. I spoke to her father myself. You know what he told me? (*He takes off the trousers and throws them at the* TAILOR. *The* TAILOR *exits.* BILLY *starts to dress in the suit he will be wearing for this and the following Scene. He puts on a shirt, vest, tie and jacket.*) The same thing he told you—he said, that his daughter went to hell ten years ago and she could stay there forever before he'd spend a cent to get her out. Isn't that what he said?

AMOS. Yes, Mr. Flynn, that's what he said. But she's my wife, Mr. Flynn, I'll pay you twenty dollars a week on my salary. (AMOS *crosses to help* BILLY *get dressed,*) I'll give you notes with interest—double, triple—Mr. Flynn—till every cent is paid. I promise ya. I promise ya.

BILLY. You know, that's touching. To care for a woman that much is really very touching. But, I've got a motto, and that motto is this—play square. Dead square. Sit down. Now, when you came to me yesterday, I didn't ask you was she guilty. I didn't ask was she innocent. I didn't ask you if she was a drunk or a dope fiend. No foolish questions like that, now did I? No. All I said was, "Have you got five thousand dollars?" And you said yes. But you haven't got five thousand dollars so I figure you're a dirty liar.

AMOS. (*Starts to take money, certificates, etc., back.*) I'm sorry, Mr. Flynn.

BILLY. (*Puts hand on money and takes it from* AMOS. *Puts it in desk drawer.*) But, I took her case and I'll keep it because I play square. Now look, Hart, I'm not a braggart. I don't like to blow my own horn, but believe me, if Jesus Christ had lived in Chicago today—and if he had five thousand dollars and had come to me—things would have turned out differently. Now, here's what we're gonna do . . . by tomorrow morning I'll have her name on the front page of every newspaper in town. She'll be a celebrity. Hottest little jazz slayer since Velma Kelly. She'll be famous, see. Then we announce we're gonna hold an auction. Tell 'em we got to raise money for her defense. They'll buy anything she ever touched —her shoes, her dresses, her perfume, her underwear. Plus, we tell 'em that if by due process of law she gets hanged . . .

AMOS. Hanged?

BILLY. . . . the stuff triples in value. And that's how we raise the rest of the five thousand dollars. I'll give you twenty percent of everything we make over that, and that's what I call playing square.

AMOS. I don't know, Mr. Flynn.

BILLY. I don't figure you got a choice. (BILLY *walks off the Winch Down Stage to Center.* ROXIE *enters from the pit stairs. Winch goes off with* AMOS. *Drum Doors close.*) You see, it's like this . . . either I get the entire five thousand . . . (*Trombone plays segue from the Bandstand. To* ROXIE.) . . . or you'll rot in jail before I bring you to trial.

ROXIE. Rot in jail? You don't really mean that, do you?

BILLY. I certainly do.

ROXIE. (*As she comes up the stairs to stage level.*) Look, Mr. Flynn, I've never been very good at this sort of thing. I've always had a great deal of trouble expressing myself. But couldn't we possibly make some sort of arrangement between us? I can be an awfully good sport.

BILLY. Hey, you mean one thing to me—five thousand bucks —and that's all. Get it? Now look, in a few minutes we're gonna have a big press conference here. There'll be a whole bunch of photographers and reporters and that sob sister from the Evening Star is coming. (*Off Stage from behind the Bandstand, we hear a coloratura trill.*) I don't figure we'll have any

trouble with her. (*Another trill.*) She'll swallow, hook, line and
sinker. Because it's what she wants. (*Another trill.* Two MEN
bring on chairs for ROXIE *and* BILLY *and exit.*) Her name's
Mary Sunshine. (*They turn their chairs to face the Bandstand Upstage.* MARY SUNSHINE *appears. She takes her place
behind the microphone on the Bandstand.*)

SONG: "A LITTLE BIT OF GOOD"

MARY SUNSHINE. (*Sung.*)
WHEN I WAS A TINY TOT
OF MAYBE TWO OR THREE
I CAN STILL REMEMBER WHAT
MY MOTHER SAID TO ME . . .

PLACE ROSE COLORED GLASSES ON YOUR NOSE
AND YOU WILL SEE THE ROBINS
NOT THE CROWS

FOR IN THE TENSE AND TANGLED WEB
OUR WEARY LIVES CAN WEAVE
YOU'RE SO MUCH BETTER OFF IF YOU
     BELIEVE . . .

THAT THERE'S A LITTLE BIT OF GOOD
IN EVERYONE
IN EVERYONE YOU'LL EVER KNOW

YES, THERE'S A LITTLE BIT OF GOOD
IN EVERYONE
THOUGH MANY TIMES, IT DOESN'T SHOW

IT ONLY TAKES THE TAKING TIME WITH ONE
     ANOTHER
FOR UNDER EVERY MEAN VENEER
THERE'S SOMEONE WARM AND DEAR
KEEP LOOKING . . .

FOR THAT BIT OF GOOD IN EVERYONE
THE ONES WE CALL BAD
ARE NEVER ALL BAD
SO TRY TO FIND THAT LITTLE BIT OF GOOD!

(*Vocalese—to:*)
IT ONLY TAKES THE TAKING TIME WITH ONE
    ANOTHER
FOR UNDER EVERY MEAN VENEER
THERE'S SOMEONE WARM AND DEAR
KEEP LOOKING . . .

FOR THAT LITTLE GOOD IN EVERYONE
ALTHOUGH YOU MEET RATS
THEY'RE NOT COMPLETE RATS
SO TRY TO FIND THAT LITTLE BIT OF GOOD!

(ROXIE *and* BILLY *rise from their seats on the last high note. They applaud as* MARY SUNSHINE *exits.* ROXIE *and* BILLY *swing their chairs around toward the audience as lights go out on the Bandstand.*)

ROXIE. Mary Sunshine is going to interview me! Holy crap!
BILLY. Hey, and pipe down on the swearin'. From here on in, you say nothin' rougher than, "Oh, dear." Get it?
ROXIE. Yes sir.
BILLY. Sit down. (ROXIE *sits.*) Now, the first thing we got to do is go after sympathy from the Press. They're not all pushovers like that Mary Sunshine. Chicago is a tough town. It's gotten so tough that they shoot the girls right out from under you. But there's one thing that they can never resist and that's a reformed sinner—so I've decided to rewrite the story of your life. It starts tomorrow in the Star. "From Convent to Jail."
ROXIE. Convent! Oh, Mr. Flynn, they'll never believe that.
BILLY. Oh, no? Get this . . . (*He begins to make up her life story on the spot.* BILLY *cues* MUSICAL CONDUCTOR. *Music under.*) Beautiful Southern home . . . Every luxury and refinement. Parents dead, educated at the Sacred Heart, fortune swept away—a run away marriage, a lovely, innocent girl, bewildered by what's happened . . . young, full of life . . (BILLY *cues music change.*) . . . lonely, you were caught up by the mad whirl of a great city—jazz, cabarets, liquor . . . (ROXIE *getting caught up, rises.*) Sit down. You were drawn

like a moth to the flame. And now the mad whirl has ceased. A butterfly crushed on the wheel. (*Music out.*) You have sinned and you are sorry.

ROXIE. God, that's beautiful.

BILLY. And cut out God, too. Stay where you're better acquainted. The important thing to remember when the reporters get here is remorse, regret. You're sorry. *Sorry.* You would give your life gladly to bring him back. Now, when they ask you why you killed him—all you can remember is a fearful quarrel and he threatened to kill you. You can still see him coming toward you with that awful look in his eyes . . . (ROXIE *can see him.*) And get this—you *both* reached for the gun. That's your grounds. Self-defense. (MATRON *enters.*)

MATRON. Mr. Flynn, the reporters are here.

BILLY. Let 'em in, Butch. (*Reminding* ROXIE.) And remember—remorse, regret, and you both reached for the gun. (*A barrage of* REPORTERS *and* MARY SUNSHINE *enter.*) Good day, gentlemen. Miss Sunshine. It's always a pleasure to see the members of the Press. You know my client, Miss Roxie Hart.

ROXIE. (*With a Southern accent.*) Ladies and gentlemen, I'm just so flattered y'all came to see me. I guess you want to know why I shot the bastard. (BILLY *grabs* ROXIE *and sits her on his knee like a ventriloquist's dummy.*)

BILLY. Sit down, dummy. (*Music up.* BILLY *sings all of* ROXIE's *responses, as she mouths them like a ventriloquist's dummy. His voice seems to come out of* ROXIE.)

BANDLEADER. (*From the Bandstand.*) Mr. Billy Flynn sings the "Press Conference Rag"—notice how his mouth never moves—almost.

SONG: "WE BOTH REACHED FOR THE GUN"

REPORTERS. (*Sung.*)
WHERE'D YOU COME FROM?
BILLY. (ROXIE.)
MISSISSIPPI
REPORTERS.
AND YOUR PARENTS?
BILLY. (ROXIE.)
VERY WEALTHY.

REPORTERS.
WHERE ARE THEY NOW?
BILLY. (ROXIE.)
SIX FEET UNDER.
BILLY.
BUT SHE WAS GRANTED ONE MORE START
BILLY. (ROXIE.)
THE CONVENT OF THE SACRED HEART!
REPORTERS.
WHEN'D YOU GET HERE?
BILLY. (ROXIE.)
1920.
REPORTERS.
HOW OLD WERE YOU?
BILLY. (ROXIE.) (ROXIE *elbows* BILLY.)
DON'T REMEMBER
REPORTERS.
THEN WHAT HAPPENED?
BILLY. (ROXIE.)
I MET AMOS
AND HE STOLE MY HEART AWAY
CONVINCED ME TO ELOPE ONE DAY
MARY SUNSHINE. (*Spoken.*) A convent girl! A run away
marriage! Oh, it's too terrible. You poor, poor dear.
REPORTERS.
WHO'S FRED CASELY?
BILLY. (ROXIE.)
MY EX-BOY FRIEND.
REPORTERS.
WHY'D YOU SHOOT HIM?
BILLY. (ROXIE.)
I WAS LEAVIN'.
REPORTERS.
WAS HE ANGRY?
BILLY. (ROXIE.)
LIKE A MADMAN!
STILL I SAID, "FRED, MOVE ALONG"
BILLY.
SHE KNEW THAT SHE WAS DOIN' WRONG
REPORTERS.
THEN DESCRIBE IT

BILLY. (ROXIE.)
HE CAME TOWARD ME.
REPORTERS.
WITH THE PISTOL?
BILLY. (ROXIE.)
FROM MY BUREAU
REPORTERS.
DID YOU FIGHT HIM?
BILLY. (ROXIE.)
LIKE A TIGER
BILLY.
HE HAD STRENGTH AND SHE HAD NONE
BILLY. (ROXIE.)
AND YET WE BOTH REACHED FOR THE GUN
OH YES, OH YES, OH YES WE BOTH
OH YES WE BOTH
OH YES, WE BOTH REACHED FOR
THE GUN, THE GUN, THE GUN, THE GUN,
OH YES, WE BOTH REACHED FOR THE GUN, FOR
THE GUN
BILLY and REPORTERS.
OH YES, OH YES, OH YES THEY BOTH
OH YES, THEY BOTH
OH YES, THEY BOTH REACHED FOR
THE GUN, THE GUN, THE GUN, THE GUN
OH YES, THEY BOTH REACHED FOR THE GUN,
    FOR
THE GUN

BILLY.
UNDERSTANDABLE
UNDERSTANDABLE
YES, IT'S PERFECTLY UNDERSTANDABLE
COMPREHENSIBLE
COMPREHENSIBLE
NOT A BIT REPREHENSIBLE
IT'S SO DEFENSIBLE!

REPORTERS.
HOW'RE YOU FEELING?

BILLY. (ROXIE.)
VERY FRIGHTENED
REPORTERS.
ARE YOU SORRY?
ROXIE. (*In her own voice.*)
ARE YOU KIDDING?
REPORTERS.
WHAT'S YOUR STATEMENT?
BILLY. (ROXIE.)
ALL I'D SAY IS
THOUGH MY CHOO-CHOO
JUMPED THE TRACK
I'D GIVE MY LIFE TO BRING
HIM BACK
REPORTERS.
AND?
BILLY. (ROXIE.)
STAY AWAY FROM
REPORTERS.
WHAT?
BILLY. (ROXIE.)
JAZZ AND LIQUOR
REPORTERS.
AND?
BILLY. (ROXIE.)
AND THE MEN WHO
REPORTERS.
WHAT?
BILLY. (ROXIE.)
PLAY FOR FUN
REPORTERS.
AND WHAT?
BILLY. (ROXIE.)
THAT'S THE THOUGHT THAT
REPORTERS.
YEAH
BILLY. (ROXIE.)
CAME UPON ME
REPORTERS.
WHEN?

BILLY. (ROXIE.)
WHEN WE BOTH REACHED FOR THE GUN!

MARY SUNSHINE.
UNDERSTANDABLE
UNDERSTANDABLE
BILLY and MARY SUNSHINE.
YES, IT'S PERFECTLY UNDERSTANDABLE
COMPREHENSIBLE
COMPREHENSIBLE
NOT A BIT REPREHENSIBLE
IT'S SO DEFENSIBLE!

BILLY.	REPORTERS.
(*Spoken.*)	OH YES, OH YES, OH YES THEY BOTH
	OH YES, THEY BOTH
Let me	OH YES, THEY BOTH REACHED FOR
hear it!	THE GUN, THE GUN, THE GUN, THE GUN
A little	OH YES, THEY BOTH REACHED FOR
louder!	THE GUN, FOR THE GUN
	OH YES, OH YES, OH YES THEY BOTH
	OH YES, THEY BOTH
	OH YES, THEY BOTH REACHED FOR
Now you	THE GUN, THE GUN, THE GUN, THE GUN
got it!	OH YES, THEY BOTH REACHED FOR THE GUN, FOR THE GUN

BILLY and REPORTERS.
OH YES, OH YES, OH YES, THEY BOTH
OH YES, THEY BOTH
OH YES, THEY BOTH REACHED FOR
THE GUN, THE GUN, THE GUN, THE GUN
OH YES, THEY BOTH REACHED FOR THE GUN,
FOR THE GUN

OH YES, OH YES, OH YES THEY BOTH
OH YES THEY BOTH

OH YES, THEY BOTH REACHED FOR
THE GUN, THE GUN, THE GUN, THE GUN
THE GUN, THE GUN, THE GUN, THE GUN
THE GUN, THE GUN, THE GUN, THE GUN
THE GUN, THE GUN, THE GUN, THE GUN

(ONE DANCER *exits and returns with a "trick" glass of milk,
    and hands it to* BILLY. BILLY *pretends to drink the milk
    as he sings the last note.* ROXIE *mimes singing the last
    note.*)

BILLY.
BOTH REACHED FOR THE GUN
    REPORTERS.
THE GUN, THE GUN, THE GUN, THE GUN
THE GUN, THE GUN, THE GUN, THE GUN
THE GUN, THE GUN, THE GUN, THE GUN
THE GUN, THE GUN, THE GUN, THE GUN
BOTH REACHED FOR THE GUN

SCENE 9

SCENE: *Limbo.*

AT RISE: ROXIE *remains Center Stage. A* GROUP OF REPORTERS
    *stand in front of her. They are telephoning their news-
    papers, using imaginary phones. We hear the sound of a
    teletype machine. Very staccato. Newspaper backdrop in.
    Music under.*

FIRST REPORTER. "STOP THE PRESSES!"
SECOND REPORTER. "CONVENT GIRL HELD!"
THIRD REPORTER. "WE BOTH REACHED FOR THE
GUN, SAYS ROXIE!"
FOURTH REPORTER. "DANCING FEET LEAD TO SOR-
ROW, SAYS BEAUTIFUL JAZZ SLAYER!"
FIFTH REPORTER. "ROXIE SOBS. I'D GIVE ANYTHING
TO BRING HIM BACK!"
SIXTH REPORTER. "JAZZ AND LIQUOR, ROXIE'S DOWN-
FALL!" Ya got that, Charlie? Right. (REPORTERS *exit, reveal-*

ing ROXIE *reading a newspaper with a headline that says,* "*ROXIE ROCKS CHICAGO.*")

ROXIE. (*To the audience.*) You wanna know something? I always wanted my name in the paper. Before Amos, I used to date this well-to-do, ugly bootlegger. He used to like to take me out and show me off. Ugly guys like to do that. Once it said in the paper, "Gangland's Al Capelli seen at Chez Vito with cute redheaded chorine." That was me. I clipped it out and saved it. (*Holds up newspaper.*) Now look, "ROXIE ROCKS CHICAGO." (*Gives the paper to* SOMEONE *in the audience. Newspaper backdrop out.*) Here, read this. Look, I'm gonna tell you the truth. Not that the truth *really* matters, but I'm gonna tell you anyway. The thing is, see . . . I'm older than I ever intended to be. All my life I wanted to be a dancer in vaudeville. Oh, yeah. Have my own act. But, no. No. No. No. They always turned me down. It was one big world full of "No." Life. Then Amos came along. Sweet, safe Amos, who never says no. You know some guys are like mirrors, and when I catch myself in Amos' face I'm always a kid. Ya could love a guy like that. Look now, I gotta tell ya, and I hope this ain't too crude. In the bed department, Amos was zero. I mean, when we went to bed, he made love to me like he was fixin' a carburetor or somethin'. "I love ya, honey. I love ya." Anyway, to make a long story short, I started foolin' around. Then I started screwin' around, which is foolin' around without dinner. I gave up the vaudeville idea, because after all those years . . . well, you sort of figure opportunity just passed you by. Oh, but it ain't. Oh no, no, no, no it ain't. If this Flynn guy gets me off, and with all this publicity, I could still get into vaudeville. I could still have my own act. Now, I got me a world full of "Yes." (*Sings:*)

SONG: "ROXIE"

THE NAME ON EVERYBODY'S LIPS
IS GONNA BE ROXIE
THE LADY RAKIN' IN THE CHIPS
IS GONNA BE ROXIE

I'M GONNA BE A CELEBRITY
THAT MEANS SOMEBODY EVERYONE KNOWS

THEY'RE GONNA RECOGNIZE MY EYES
MY HAIR, MY TEETH, MY BOOBS, MY NOSE

FROM JUST SOME DUMB MECHANIC'S WIFE
I'M GONNA BE ROXIE
WHO SAYS THAT MURDER'S NOT AN ART?

AND WHO IN CASE SHE DOESN'T HANG
CAN SAY SHE STARTED WITH A BANG?
ROXIE HART!

(*Spoken.*) I'm going to have a swell act, too! Yeah, I'll get a boy to work with—someone who can lift me and smile at me— Oh, hell, I'll get two boys. It'll frame me better! Think "Big," Roxie— I'll get a whole bunch of boys. (Six Boys *enter and begin to dance with* Roxie. Roxie *sings:*)

THE NAME ON EVERYBODY'S LIPS
IS GONNA BE
  Boys.
ROXIE
  Roxie.
THE LADY RAKIN' IN THE CHIPS
IS GONNA BE
  Boys.
ROXIE
  Roxie.
SHE'S GONNA BE A CELEBRITY
  Roxie.
THAT MEANS SOMEBODY EVERYONE KNOWS
  Boys.
THEY'RE GONNA RECOGNIZE HER EYES
HER HAIR, HER TEETH
  Roxie.
MY BOOBS, MY NOSE
FROM JUST SOME DUMB MECHANIC'S WIFE
I'M GONNA BE
  Boys.
ROXIE
  Roxie.
WHO SAYS THAT MURDER'S NOT AN ART?
  Boys.
AND WHO IN CASE SHE DOESN'T HANG

ROXIE.
CAN SAY SHE STARTED WITH A BANG?
    ROXIE and Boys.
FOXY ROXIE HART
    Boys.
THEY'RE GONNA WAIT OUTSIDE IN LINE
TO GET TO SEE ROXIE
    ROXIE.
THINK OF THOSE AUTOGRAPHS I'LL SIGN
"GOOD LUCK TO YOU" ROXIE

AND I'LL APPEAR IN A LAVALIERE
THAT GOES ALL THE WAY DOWN TO MY WAIST
    Boys.
HERE A RING, THERE A RING
EVERYWHERE A RING A LING
    ROXIE.
BUT ALWAYS IN THE BEST OF TASTE
(*Spoken.*)
Ooo, I'm a star.
    BOY No. 1. (*Spoken.*)
And the audience loves her.
    ROXIE. (*Spoken.*)
And I love the audience
    BOY No. 2. (*Spoken.*)
And the audience loves her for loving them
    ROXIE. (*Spoken.*)
And I love the audience for loving me.
    BOY No. 3. (*Spoken.*)
And they just love each other.
    ROXIE. (*Spoken.*)
And that's because none of us got enough love in our child-
    hood.
    Boys. (*All. Spoken.*)
That's right.
    ROXIE. (*Spoken.*)
And that's show biz, kid.
    Boys. (*Spoken.*)
Oh yeah.

(*Dance.*)

Roxie. (*Sung.*)
AND SOPHIE TUCKER'LL SHIT, I KNOW
TO SEE HER NAME GET BILLED BELOW
ALL.
FOXY ROXIE HART!
Boys.
CHUH, CHUH, CHUH, ETC. . .

(*The* Boys *split and exit Stage Right and Stage Left, dancing.* Roxie *dances alone Upstage Center.*)

Roxie. (*Spoken, watching the* Boys *dance off.*) Those are my boys. (*With her back to the audience, she makes a gesture of farewell and exits into Center Drum. Doors close as LIGHTS—*)

BLACKOUT

Announcer. (*Reading headlines off stage. Music under.*) "ROXIE ROCKS CHICAGO!" "FANS RIOT AT ROXIE AUCTION!" ROXIE'S NIGHTIE RAISES 200 BUCKS!"

Scene 10

Scene: *In the Jail.*

At Rise: Matron *rides* s. l. *Winch in. She is seated at a table reading a newspaper.* Velma *comes up the pit stairs. She sees the headline on the* Matron's *paper—"ROXIE ROCKS CHICAGO."*

Velma. Mama, you know that I am not a jealous person, but every time I see that tomato's name on the front page—it drives me nertz.
Matron. Sit down, Baby, I got some bad news.
Velma. What do you mean?
Matron. I mean, the tour . . . the whole tour . . . it's down the drain . . . it's cancelled. Out. (*She offers* Velma *a drink from her flask.*) Here, kiddo.

VELMA. (*Takes a drink.*) Cancelled.

MATRON. Well, your name hasn't been in the papers for a long time. I been getting calls from the boys at William Morris all day. We've lost interest. We've lost interest. We don't want her. She's washed up. She's finished. She's a bum. Do you know how it hurts Mama to hear that about someone she cares for?

VELMA. Oh, sure.

MATRON. All you read about today is the Hart kid. She's hot. (VELMA *takes another swig from the flask.*)

VELMA. Hey, Mama, I've got an idea. Suppose I talk Hart into doing that sister act with me?

MATRON. (*Leaning forward.*) Well, that's what I call using the old Kanoodle. (*Music. Winch starts off.* VELMA *crosses stage. Stops Center.*)

SCENE 11

SCENE: *Limbo and* ROXIE'S *cell.*

AT RISE: VELMA *crosses Center.*

BANDLEADER. (*From the Bandstand.*) Ladies and gentlemen, Miss Velma Kelly in an act of desperation. (VELMA *bows.* S. R. *Winch comes in.* ROXIE *is seated at a table in her cell, eating.*)

SONG: "I CAN'T DO IT ALONE"

VELMA. (*Sung to* ROXIE.)
MY SISTER AND I HAD AN ACT THAT COULDN'T
    FLOP
MY SISTER AND I WERE HEADED STRAIGHT
    FOR THE TOP
MY SISTER AND I EARNED A THOU A WEEK
    AT LEAST
BUT MY SISTER IS NOW, UNFORTUNATELY,
    DECEASED

I KNOW, IT'S SAD, OF COURSE, BUT A FACT
IS STILL A FACT
AND NOW ALL THAT REMAINS
IS THE REMAINS OF A PERFECT DOUBLE ACT!

(ROXIE *yawns. Spoken:*) Do you know that you are exactly
the same size as my sister? You would fit in her wardrobe perfectly. Look, why don't I show you some of the act, huh?
Watch this. (VELMA *begins to perform the act, doing both
parts. Music up strong.*) Now, you have to imagine it with two
people. It's swell with two people. (*Sung.*)
FIRST I'D . . .
THEN SHE'D . . .

THEN WE'D . . .
BUT I CAN'T DO IT ALONE!
THEN SHE'D . . .
THEN I'D . . .
THEN WE'D . . .
BUT I CAN'T DO IT ALONE!

SHE'D SAY, "WHAT'S YOUR SISTER LIKE?"
I'D SAY, "MEN," YUK, YUK, YUK
SHE'D SAY, "YOU'RE THE CAT'S MEOW"
THEN WE'D WOW THE CROWD AGAIN
WHEN SHE'D GO . . .
I'D GO . . .
WE'D GO . . .

AND THEN THOSE DING DONG DADDIES
        STARTED TO ROAR
WHISTLED, STOMPED, AND STAMPED ON THE
        FLOOR
YELLING, SCREAMING, BEGGING FOR MORE.
(*Spoken.*) And we'd say, "O.K. fellas, keep your socks up.
You ain't seen nothin' yet!" (VELMA *dances, builds to a big
finish. Sung:*)
BUT I SIMPLY CANNOT DO IT ALONE
(*She stands, exhausted, in front of* ROXIE. *VAMP continues
under. Spoken:*) Well? What did ya think? Come on, you
can say. (ROXIE *gives her a raspberry.*) O.K., O.K. The first
part can always be rewritten. But the second part was really
nifty. Watch this. (*Begins the act again. Sung:*)
THEN SHE'D . . .
THEN I'D . . .
THEN WE'D . . .
BUT I CAN'T DO IT ALONE!

SHE'D SAY, "WHAT STATE'S CHICAGO IN?"
I'D SAY, "ILL" DID YA GET THAT?
SHE'D SAY, "TURN YOUR MOTOR OFF"
    (*Wild break.*)
I CAN HEAR 'EM CHEERIN' STILL

WHEN SHE'D GO . . .
I'D GO . . .
WE'D GO . . .
AND THEN THOSE TWO-BIT JOHNNIES DID IT
    UP BROWN
TO CHEER THE BEST ATTRACTION IN TOWN
THEY NEARLY TORE THE BALCONY DOWN
(*Spoken.*) And we'd say, "O.K. boys, we're goin' home, but
here's a few more partin' shots!" And this . . . this we did
in perfect unison. (*The dance is even more frantic than before.
To . . . Sung:*)
NOW, YOU'VE SEEN ME GOIN' THROUGH IT
IT MAY SEEM THERE'S NOTHIN' TO IT
BUT I SIMPLY CANNOT DO IT ALONE!
(*She stands before* ROXIE, *truly exhausted. Spoken:*) Ah,
well . . . ?

ROXIE. (*Rising, unimpressed.*) Boy, they sure got lousy
floor shows in jails now-a-days . . . (*She starts off.*) I mean,
there was a time when you could go to jail and get a really . . .

VELMA. O.K. Roxie! I'll level with ya. (ROXIE *stops and
turns.*)

ROXIE. Listen, I don't want to hear it. You think you're
foolin' me? What did Mama just tell ya? That you're old
news? Washed up? It's me they want now, huh? Do you remember the time I asked you for advice and you said, "I don't
get any advice and I don't give any advice." So who needs
this corny sister bit? And I'll tell you something else. Your
friend Mama—she wanted to make some phone calls for me.
Do you know what I told her? I don't need you. And I'm
telling you the same thing. I don't need anybody. Haven't
you read the papers lately? I'm a star— I'm a big star *single*.
(ROXIE *starts to exit again.*)

VELMA. Thanks.

ROXIE. Nothin' personal, you understand. Nothin' personal.
(ROXIE *exits.*)

VELMA. Nothin' personal. Nothin's ever personal. (*Music up.* VELMA *crosses to a Cut-out of a man and woman in bed. Puts her head in woman's section. Man's head is missing. Sung:*)

LIKE THE DESERTED BRIDE ON HER WEDDING
    NIGHT
ALL ALONE AND SHAKING WITH FRIGHT
WITH HER BRAND NEW HUBBY NOWHERE IN
    SIGHT . . .
I SIMPLY CANNOT DO IT ALONE . . .

(*Cut-out moves off as lights fade on* VELMA *and come up on the* BANDLEADER *on the Bandstand.*)

BANDLEADER. (*Spoken.*) At the tone the time will be 12:00 A.M. (*A tone from the* ORCHESTRA.) And now for all you Chicago stay-up-laters, you night owls who only come alive after dark, we dedicate this next tune. "Chicago After Midnight."

(*The* ORCHESTRA *starts to play as the lights go down on the Bandstand. The lights come up on the* MATRON s. L., *music continues under.* ["CHICAGO AFTER MID-NIGHT."])

SCENE 12

SCENE: *Limbo and a bedroom, somewhere in Chicago.*

AT RISE: *The* MATRON *addresses the audience.*

MATRON. (*Begins narration.*) Well, here's the way I got the story. There's this Kitty—something or other. I didn't catch her last name. Anyway, she's some sort of heiress. Her folks are in pineapples, grapefruits, somethin' like that. Well, she's playing house in a Northside apartment with a guy by the name of Harry. Harry spends all his time in bed. You know, a real mattress dancer . . . (*Drum Doors open. A Bed rolls down stage on the Center Winch. We see the bottom of*

HARRY's feet.) What Harry does for a living nobody is quite sure, but it don't matter because she's footin' all the bills— paying for everything. Anyhoo, last night this Kitty dame comes home . . . (A BEAUTIFUL GIRL [GO-TO-HELL KITTY] enters. *She crosses to the bed and looks at* HARRY's *feet.*) Harry's already in bed—which is par for the course for Harry. She goes to change . . . (KITTY *exits for a moment and returns.*) And when she returns, she notices something rather odd . . . (TWO WOMEN's FEET *appear in the bed next to* HARRY. TWO MORE WOMEN's FEET *appear next to* HARRY's *feet in the bed a beat later.*) Extremely odd . . . puzzled—she disappears for a second. (KITTY *exits again and returns with a tommy gun.*) When she returns she gently awakens Harry . . . (MATRON *exits.*)

KITTY. Oh, Harry . . . (*The* MAN *wakes up. So do the* TWO GIRLS *in the bed with him.*)

HARRY. (*Very reasonably.*) O.K. Are you gonna believe what you see or what I tell you?

KITTY. What I see! (*She guns* HARRY *and the* GIRLS *down. Music out. They die in slow motion.*)

BANDLEADER. Goodnight, folks. (*Music up.*)

BLACKOUT

ANNOUNCER. (*Reading headlines Off Stage.*) "LAKE SHORE DRIVE MASSACRE!" "BERSERK FILLY FELLS THREE!" "THREE IN BED—ALL DEAD!"

SCENE 13

SCENE: *The Jail.*

AT RISE: PHOTOGRAPHERS, REPORTERS, MARY SUNSHINE, *the* MATRON *and* BILLY FLYNN *enter. The* S. L. *and* S. R. *Winches roll on.* ROXIE *sits in her cell on* S. R. *Winch.* VELMA *sits in her cell on* S. L. *Winch. They watch the following:*

BILLY *is hanging on to* GO-TO-HELL KITTY. *She is in a strait-jacket, and is a reluctant heroine—kicking at the* MEN *trying to take her picture.*

BILLY. (*To* REPORTERS.) Gentlemen, please, my client will be happy to answer all your questions . . . (KITTY *bites him.*) Ow, will you stop biting? I'll get hydrophobia.

KITTY. Go to hell. (*The* REPORTERS *all ask questions. "Now, Miss Katz . . . etc."*) Go to hell all of you. I'm not answering any more questions.

BILLY. Please direct your questions to her counsel.

KITTY. You're not my counsel, and I want my money back.

BILLY. It's not your money. It's your *mother's* money.

KITTY. (*Goes for* BILLY'S *groin with her knee.*) Get out of here, ya fop.

ROXIE. (*Calls across the room.*) Oh, Miss Sunshine . . .

MARY SUNSHINE. (*Hears her.*) Not now, Roxie.

(REPORTERS *move in around* KITTY.)

FIRST REPORTER. Oh, Miss Katz, did you know those two ladies personally?

KITTY. (*Smiling.*) Did I know those two ladies personally? Was that your question?

FIRST REPORTER. Yes, that's my question. (KITTY *knees him in the groin. He hops off.*)

MARY SUNSHINE. Oh, she's very high spirited, isn't she?

MATRON. (*To* KITTY.) Come on, dearie. I'm gonna show you to your suite. You're gonna love it. (MATRON *leads* KITTY *and* REPORTERS *into Center Drum.* BILLY *starts to follow them Upstage.*)

BILLY. (*Directing the* REPORTERS *Upstage.*) Step right in here, gentlemen. She will answer all your questions and afterwards I'll be happy to give you an interview myself . . .

ROXIE. (*Screaming after* BILLY.) Mr. Flynn! Mr. Flynn!

(BILLY *reluctantly walks over to* ROXIE. *He is anxious to get into the room with the* REPORTERS.)

BILLY. Hi, Trixie, I mean, Roxie. Boy, what a hellion, huh? And a socialite, too! Her mother owns all the pineapples in Hawaii.

ROXIE. What the hell do I care about pineapples? Did ya get my trial date?

BILLY. Take it easy, kid. I'll get to it. I'll get to it. (VELMA *stops him on his way back to* KITTY.)

VELMA. Mr. Flynn. There's a couple of things I'd like to discuss about *my* trial, too.

BILLY. (*Stopping momentarily.*) Oh yeah . . . Hi ya, Velma. First things first, honey. (*Walking away.*) I'll get to it. I'll get to it. (BILLY *exits into the Center Drum. Ad lib:*) All right, gentlemen. All right . . . (*Drum doors close.*)

ROXIE. (*To herself.*) Pineapples. I got a feeling you're in trouble, Roxie.

VELMA. (*To herself.*) Socialite. You lose again, Velma.

ROXIE. (*To herself.*) There's only one person who can help you now, Roxie.

VELMA. (*To herself.*) There's only one person you can count on now, Velma.

BANDLEADER. (*From the Bandstand.*) And now, Miss Roxie Hart and Miss Velma Kelly sing a song of unrelenting determination and unmitigated ego.

(ROXIE *and* VELMA *rise, put on raincoats and hats and walk Center Stage. They turn forward and walk Down Stage, and sit back-to-back on the lip of the stage.*)

SONG: "MY OWN BEST FRIEND"

ROXIE and VELMA. (*Sung.*)
ONE THING I KNOW
ROXIE.
AND I'VE ALWAYS KNOWN
VELMA. (*Sung a beat behind* ROXIE's *lyrics.*)
I'VE ALWAYS KNOWN
ROXIE.
I AM MY OWN BEST FRIEND
VELMA.
   I AM MY OWN BEST FRIEND
ROXIE.
BABY'S ALIVE
VELMA.
   BABY'S ALIVE
ROXIE.
BUT BABY'S ALONE

VELMA.
  BUT BABY'S ALONE
ROXIE.
AND BABY'S HER OWN BEST FRIEND
VELMA.
  AND BABY'S HER OWN BEST FRIEND
ROXIE and VELMA.
MANY'S THE GUY
WHO TOLD ME HE CARES
BUT THEY WERE SCRATCHIN' MY BACK
'CAUSE I WAS SCRATCHIN' THEIRS
ROXIE.
AND TRUSTING TO LUCK
VELMA.
  AND TRUSTING TO LUCK
ROXIE.
THAT'S ONLY FOR FOOLS
VELMA.
  ONLY FOR FOOLS
ROXIE.
I PLAY IN A GAME
VELMA.
  I PLAY IN A GAME
ROXIE.
WHERE I MAKE THE RULES
VELMA.
  WHERE I MAKE THE RULES
ROXIE and VELMA.
AND RULE NUMBER ONE
FROM HERE TO THE END
IS I AM MY OWN BEST FRIEND

THREE MUSKETEERS
  (CHORUS *hums in the background.*)
WHO NEVER SAY DIE
  (CHORUS *hums louder in the background.*)
ARE STANDING HERE THIS MINUTE
VELMA.
ME

Roxie.
ME
Velma.
MYSELF
Roxie.
MYSELF
Velma.
AND I

(Chorus: *"AND I, AND I, AND I, AND I, I, I"* in the *background, Off Stage. Two* Girls *enter on the Bandstand with hats full of confetti. They throw confetti on* Roxie *and* Velma.)

Roxie and Velma.
IF LIFE IS A SCHOOL
(Chorus *hums.*)
I'LL PASS EVERY TEST
(Chorus *hums.*)
IF LIFE IS A GAME
(Chorus *hums.*)
I'LL PLAY IT THE BEST
(Chorus *hums.*)
'CAUSE I WON'T GIVE IN
AND I'LL NEVER BEND
AND I AM MY OWN BEST FRIEND

(Chorus *hums a big finish. The* Two Girls *on the Bandstand exit.* Roxie *and* Velma *run off dramatically, to opposite sides of the stage. They run back onto the stage, as if taking a bow.* Velma *bows.* Roxie *faints.*)

Velma. (*Looking at* Roxie *lying on the floor.*) What the hell was that?

Roxie. (*Lifting her head a little to call the press.*) Mr. Flynn? Miss Sunshine? And all you reporters! (*She faints again. Drum Doors open and* Mary Sunshine *and* Billy Flynn *rush on. They surround* Roxie. *Ad lib: "What's happened to her." "Roxie?" "Mrs. Hart?", etc. Finally,* Roxie *lifts her head.*)

Roxie. Oh, don't worry about me. It's just that I'm going to have a baby. (*Chord.*)

All. A baby! (Reporters *"freeze."*)

VELMA. Shit.

BILLY. (*Over* REPORTERS, *as he exits.*) I want the best doctor in the city for my poor client. Somebody pick that girl up.

(REPORTERS *come out of "freeze."* BILLY *exits.* ROXIE *and* REPORTERS *continue hub-bub,* VELMA *and* ROXIE *exchange looks.* ROXIE *laughs.* VELMA *smiles, and starts off.*)

VELMA. (*Sung.*)
AND ALL THAT JAZZ!

(*Flashbulbs pop. Everyone is talking to* ROXIE *at once. She is loving it as the—*)

CURTAIN FALLS

ACT TWO

SCENE 1

SCENE: *The Jail.*

AT RISE: *VAMP from the* ORCHESTRA.

REPORTERS *are discovered on both sides of the stage talking into imaginary phones. They anxiously await the "news" about* ROXIE.

VELMA *appears on the Bandstand looking down.* BILLY FLYNN *stands Stage Left.*

VELMA. (*To the audience.*) Hello suckers, welcome back. (*Pointing down.*) Roxie's in there being looked over by the State Medical Examiner. She says she's gonna have a baby. Now why didn't I think of that?

SONG: "I KNOW A GIRL"

(*Sung.*)
CAN YOU IMAGINE?
I MEAN, CAN YOU IMAGINE?

CAN YOU BELIEVE IT?
I MEAN, CAN YOU BELIEVE IT?

I KNOW A GIRL

A GIRL WHO LANDS ON TOP
YOU COULD PUT HER FACE INTO A PAIL OF
    SLOP
AND SHE'D COME UP SMELLING LIKE A ROSE
HOW SHE DOES IT, HEAVEN KNOWS.
    SECOND REPORTER. (*Into his imaginary phone.*) Hold on Charlie, she's comin' out now. (*A* DOCTOR *rolls* ROXIE *out in a wheelchair.*) Well, Doc, is she or isn't she?
    VELMA. (*Looks down.*) She is.

SECOND REPORTER. (*Into phone.*) Charlie, she is. (*Hangs up. REPORTERS "freeze."*)

VELMA. (*Sung.*)
I KNOW A GIRL
A GIRL WITH SO MUCH LUCK
SHE COULD GET RUN OVER BY A TWO-TON
    TRUCK
THEN BRUSH HERSELF OFF AND WALK AWAY
HOW SHE DOES IT, COULDN'T SAY

(REPORTERS *come out of "freeze." BILLY FLYNN crosses to DOCTOR and leads him s. l. ROXIE answers the REPORTERS' questions in mime.*)

BILLY. Doc, would you swear to that statement in court?
DOCTOR. Yes.
BILLY. Good . . . uh . . . button your fly. (BILLY *and the DOCTOR exit.*)

VELMA. (*Sung.*)
WHILST I
ON THE OTHER HAND
PUT MY FACE IN A PAIL OF SLOP
AND I WOULD SMELL LIKE A PAIL OF SLOP
I
ON THE OTHER HAND
GET RUN OVER BY A TRUCK
AND I AM DEADER THAN A DUCK

I KNOW A GIRL
WHO TELLS SO MANY LIES
ANYTHING THAT'S TRUE WOULD TRULY CROSS
    HER EYES
BUT WHAT THAT MOUSE IS SELLING
THE WHOLE WORLD BUYS
AND NOBODY SMELLS A RAT.

ROXIE. (*To the REPORTERS.*) Please, ladies and gentlemen of the press—leave the two of us alone so we can rest.

VELMA. (*Spoken.*) The two of us? (*Sung.*)
CAN YOU IMAGINE?
I MEAN, CAN YOU IMAGINE?

(REPORTERS *start to exit. Ad lib: "Of course." "Sorry, we disturbed you," etc.* EVERY REPORTER, *except one, exits. He hangs back.*)

THIRD REPORTER. Could I have one last picture please?
ROXIE. (*Smiling.*) Sure, anything for the press.

(REPORTER *snaps the picture and exits.*)

VELMA.
DO YOU BELIEVE IT?
I MEAN, DO YOU BELIEVE IT?
ROXIE. (*Sitting in the wheelchair,* ROXIE *sings ad-lib.*)
MY DEAR LITTLE BABY
VELMA. (*Sung, mocking* ROXIE.)
My dear little baby
ROXIE.
MY SWEET LITTLE BABY
VELMA.
My sweet little baby

(VELMA, *disgusted, turns Upstage on Bandstand. Lights out on Bandstand.*)

SONG: "ME AND MY BABY"*

ROXIE. (*Sung.*)
LOOK AT MY BABY AND ME

(ROXIE *rises from her wheelchair, takes off her examination garment. She is wearing a typically 'Eddie Cantor' outfit. Pants too short, white socks, bow tie. The number is sung a la Eddie.* ROXIE *performs the number with two male dancers.*)

ME AND MY BABY
MY BABY AND ME
WE'RE 'BOUT AS HAPPY AS BABIES CAN BE
WHAT IF I FIND

THAT I'M CAUGHT IN A STORM?
I DON'T CARE
MY BABY'S THERE
AND BABY'S BOUND TO KEEP ME WARM
WE'RE STICKING TOGETHER
AND AIN'T WE GOT FUN
SO MUCH TOGETHER
YOU'D COUNT US AS ONE
TELL OLD MAN WORRY TO GO CLIMB A TREE
'CAUSE I'VE GOT MY BABY
I'M WITH MY BABY
LOOK AT MY BABY AND ME

(*MUSIC continues.* ROXIE *dances. In an isolated area, on the Bandstand, we see* MARY SUNSHINE.)

MARY SUNSHINE. (*Spoken over Music while* ROXIE *dances.*) I don't see how you could possibly delay the trial another second, Mr. Flynn. My readers wouldn't stand for it. The poor child! To have her baby born in a jail! (*Lights out on* MARY SUNSHINE. ROXIE, *as she dances, is clapping her hands like Cantor. It is as if she is applauding* MARY. *Lights up on* BILLY FLYNN *in another isolated area* S. R.)

BILLY FLYNN. I can assure you she'll come to trial at the earliest possible moment. And you can quote me on that. (*Lights out on* BILLY FLYNN. *Lights up on* AMOS *on the pit stairs.*)

AMOS. Hey, everybody. I'm the father! I'm the father! (*Lights down on* AMOS. ROXIE *sings.*)

LOOKA AT MY BABY
MY BABY AND ME
A DREAM OF A DUO
NOW DON'T YOU AGREE?
WHY KEEP IT MUM
WHEN THERE'S NOTHING TO HIDE?
AND WHAT I FEEL
I MUST REVEAL
IT'S MORE THAN I CAN KEEP INSIDE
AND I CAN ASSURE YOU
IT WON'T GO AWAY

LET ME ASSURE YOU
IT GROWS EVERY DAY
I WAS A ONE ONCE
BUT NOW I'M A 'WE'
'CAUSE I GOT MY BABY
MY DEAR LITTLE BABY
LOOKA MY BABY AND ME

(ROXIE *continues dancing. Lights up on* MATRON *as the drum doors open.*)

MATRON. I think it's sweet. Real sweet, I call it. First time we ever had one of our girls knocked up. (MATRON *exits back into Drum with wheelchair. Doors close as lights go down on her area. Lights come up on* BILLY *in another area.*)

BILLY. (*Looking straight ahead as* ROXIE *dances.*) I've got it and it's brilliant. I'm gonna get Amos to divôrce you. That way all the sympathy will go to you—not him. You'll be the poor, little deserted mother-to-be and that crumb is running out on you. (*Lights go down on* BILLY. *Men dancers enter dressed as 'babies' [in diapers] in the form of an old vaudeville routine. They dance and sing with* ROXIE.)

ROXIE and BOYS. (*Sung.*)
LOOKA MY BABY
MY BABY AND ME
FACING THE WORLD
OPTIMISTICALLY
NOTHING CAN STOP US
SO, NOBODY TRY
'CAUSE BABY'S ROUGH
AND FULL OF STUFF
AND INCIDENTALLY, SO AM I
GET OUT OF OUR WAY, FOLKS
AND GIVE US SOME ROOM
WATCH HOW WE BUBBLE
AND BLOSSOM AND BLOOM
LIFE WAS A PRISON
BUT WE GOT THE KEY
ME AND MY BABY
MY DEAR LITTLE BABY
MY CUTE LITTLE BABY
MY SWEET LITTLE BABY

MY FAT LITTLE BABY
MY SOFT LITTLE BABY
MY PINK LITTLE BABY
MY BALD LITTLE BABY
LOOKA MY BABY AND ME

(ROXIE *and* BOYS *dance to finish and exit. Lights up on* AMOS,
still in the pit stairs.)

AMOS. (*Looks around, weakly.*) I'm the father! Papa! Dad-
dikins! Dada! (*As he climbs the stairs to the stage level, we
notice he wears clown flap shoes.*) Did you hear me? Did
you? No, you didn't hear me. Nobody ever hears me. (*A
GIRL enters with a hat rack on which there is a frock coat, a
celluloid collar and a top hat. She holds a pair of gloves. She
helps AMOS into all of these, then exits. He continues speaking
to the audience, as he does, his speech becomes noticeably
slower and more like Bert Williams.*) That's the story of my
life. Nobody ever listens to me. Have you noticed that at all?
Have you seen it? Am I making it up? Nobody ever knows
I'm around. Nobody. Ever. Not even my parents noticed me.
One day I went to school and when I came home, they'd
moved. (*Music up.*)

SCENE 2

SCENE: *Limbo.*

AT RISE: AMOS *stands alone in a dim spotlight.*

SONG: "MISTER CELLOPHANE"

AMOS. (*Sung.*)
IF SOMEONE STOOD UP IN A CROWD
AND RAISED HIS VOICE UP WAY OUT LOUD
AND WAVED HIS ARM
AND SHOOK HIS LEG
YOU'D NOTICE HIM

IF SOMEONE IN A MOVIE SHOW
YELLED "FIRE IN THE SECOND ROW,
THIS WHOLE PLACE IS A POWDER KEG!"
YOU'D NOTICE HIM

AND EVEN WITHOUT CLUCKING LIKE A HEN
EVERYONE GETS NOTICED, NOW AND THEN,
UNLESS, OF COURSE, THAT PERSONAGE SHOULD
    BE
INVISIBLE, INCONSEQUENTIAL ME!

CELLOPHANE
MISTER CELLOPHANE
SHOULD HAVE BEEN MY NAME
MISTER CELLOPHANE
'CAUSE YOU CAN LOOK RIGHT THROUGH ME
WALK RIGHT BY ME
AND NEVER KNOW I'M THERE!

I TELL YA
CELLOPHANE
MISTER CELLOPHANE
SHOULD HAVE BEEN MY NAME
MISTER CELLOPHANE
'CAUSE YOU CAN LOOK RIGHT THROUGH ME
WALK RIGHT BY ME
AND NEVER KNOW I'M THERE . . .

(*Music continues under as Center Drum Door opens and*
    BILLY FLYNN'S *office rolls in.* BILLY *is seated behind the*
    desk, reading a paper. AMOS *walks into the office.*)

BILLY. (*Spoken.*) Oh, Andy. I didn't see you. Sit down. Sit
down. (AMOS *sits.*) Look, Andy, I'm afraid I gotta hit you
hard. I can only hope you'll be big about it.
    AMOS. (*Slightly irritated.*) Amos. My name is Amos.
    BILLY. Who said it wasn't? It's the kid's name I'm thinkin'
about.
    AMOS. What kid?
    BILLY. Roxie's kid. You know when she's due? Early Fall.
September. Can you count? September. That means you
couldn't possibly be . . . But I want you to pass out those
cigars anyway. I don't want you to give a damn when people . . .
    AMOS. When people what?

BILLY. Laugh.

AMOS. Laugh? Why would they laugh?

BILLY. Because they can count. Can *you* count? Early Fall? (*He takes out a paper.*) Here's a copy of Roxie's first statement. It says she hadn't copulated with you for four months prior to the . . . incident.

AMOS. That's right. We hadn't done no copulating for four months . . . early Fall. Now, wait a minute. (*He has his head back, eyes on ceiling, lost in calculation.*)

BILLY. But I want you to forget all that! My client needs your support.

AMOS. (*Bitterly.*) Well . . . (*Still counting.*) . . . that don't figure out right. I couldn't be the father.

BILLY. (*Jumping up.*) Divorce her? *Is that what you said? My God man, you wouldn't divorce her! Over a little thing like that* . . . (*Softly, close to his ear.*) . . . would ya?

AMOS. (*Standing.*) *You're damned right. I'll divorce her! That's what I'll do. I'll divorce her* . . . (*To audience, after a beat.*) She probably won't even notice.

(BILLY *has seated himself during the above—goes back to newspaper. Finally, he looks up.*)

BILLY. Are you still here, Andy? I thought you'd gone.

AMOS. Yeah, I'm still here. I think. (BLACKOUT *on* BILLY's *office. Center Winch moves back. Drum Doors close.* AMOS *walks forward to the audience again. Sung.*)
SUPPOSE YOU WAS A LITTLE CAT
RESIDIN' IN A PERSON'S FLAT
WHO FED YOU FISH AND SCRATCHED YOUR
    EARS?
YOU'D NOTICE HIM

SUPPOSE YOU WAS A WOMAN WED
AND SLEEPIN' IN A DOUBLE BED
BESIDE ONE MAN FOR SEVEN YEARS
YOU'D NOTICE HIM

A HUMAN BEING'S MADE OF MORE THAN AIR
WITH ALL THAT BULK, YOU'RE BOUND TO SEE
    HIM THERE

UNLESS THAT HUMAN BEIN' NEXT TO YOU
IS UNIMPRESSIVE, UNDISTINGUISHED
YOU KNOW WHO . . .

(*Music to:*)

SHOULD HAVE BEEN MY NAME
MISTER CELLOPHANE
'CAUSE YOU CAN LOOK RIGHT THROUGH ME
WALK RIGHT BY ME
AND NEVER KNOW I'M THERE . . .
I TELL YA
CELLOPHANE
MISTER CELLOPHANE
SHOULD HAVE BEEN MY NAME
MISTER CELLOPHANE
'CAUSE YOU CAN LOOK RIGHT THROUGH ME
WALK RIGHT BY ME
AND NEVER KNOW I'M THERE
NEVER EVEN KNOW I'M THERE
(*Spoken.*) Hope I didn't take up too much of your time. (*He walks off, as the LIGHTS DIM.*)

SCENE 3

SCENE: *The Jail.*

AT RISE: *Center Drum Doors open. The Winch comes forward.* VELMA, JUNE, ANNIE, *and the* MATRON *are seated playing cards around a table.* KITTY *watches over their shoulders. A* MASTER OF CEREMONIES *steps off the Winch. Drum roll. Music under.*

MASTER OF CEREMONIES. Ladies and gentlemen, the poker game. (*He exits.*)

(*The following scene is played in pantomime:* KITTY *lights* ANNIE'S *cigar and the* MATRON *finishes dealing the cards. As they are looking at their cards, the* MATRON *coughs,* ANNIE *scratches her head,* JUNE *sniffles, and* VELMA *takes*

a long draw on her cigarette. EVERYONE *bets, then asks
for new cards in pantomime.* ANNIE *wants two cards.*
JUNE *wants three.* VELMA *wants one card and they all
look at her suspiciously. The* MATRON *wants three cards.
They all pretend to study their new cards.* KITTY *watches
them and takes the following in: The* MATRON *rises off
her chair a little with a cough to cover stealing a card
that she was sitting on. She places the new card in her
hand and glances around to see if her cheating was noticed.*
ANNIE *scratches her head and lifts her wig to get a card
stashed there. She puts the card in her hand and glances
around.* JUNE *sniffles and blows her nose hard, taking a
card out of her handkerchief. She glances around.* VELMA
*takes a draw on her cigarette and puts it in the ashtray
on the table. Bringing her hand back to her mouth, she
pulls a card out of her mouth and puts it in her hand
glancing around to see if anyone noticed.* ANNIE *starts
the next bet and* EVERYONE *puts money in the pot. Music
out.*)

ANNIE. (*Showing her hand.*) Straight. King high.

JUNE. (*Topping her, showing her hand.*) Heart flush.

VELMA. (*Topping her, showing her hand.*) Four aces.
(*They all look at the* MATRON *for a long time.*)

MATRON. (*Finally.*) Royal flush.

VELMA. A royal flush. Now where in hell did you get a royal
flush?

MATRON. The same place you got four aces. (BILLY *enters.
Music seque.*)

BILLY. (*To the* MATRON.) Hey, Diesel, get Roxie for me,
will ya?

(MATRON *exits, counting her money,* VELMA *crosses to* BILLY.
The OTHER GIRLS *start another poker game.*)

VELMA. Billy, am I glad to see you. Look, March 5th is only
a few weeks away and I've been makin' plans.

BILLY. Yeah, well, Velma . . .

VELMA. (*Takes box from under the table and crosses to*
BILLY.) Look. (*She opens the box and takes out a pair of
silver shoes with rhinestone buckles.*) For the trial. You like
'em? You like the rhinestones?

BILLY. Very nice.

VELMA. I'll wear something else if you don't.

BILLY. Look, kid, your trial date's been set back . . .

VELMA. (*Disappointed.*) Oh, no . . .

BILLY. Only 'til April 2nd. A month more.

VELMA. (*Protesting.*) But, Billy! I been makin' all these plans . . .

BILLY. Less than a month. I had to, sweetie.

VELMA. (*Putting shoes back in the box.*) And who got my date as if I didn't know, Roxie Hart?

BILLY. Hey, there's a lot of pressure on me. She's having a baby, f'chrissakes.

VELMA. Yeah, tell me about it. Listen Flynn, I had five thousand dollars, too, and sooner . . . and ah, what the hell . . . I'll be glad to get rid of her. (VELMA *crosses to put the shoe box on the table and sits down.*)

BILLY. Where is she anyway?

VELMA. Lookin' over her presents. You ought to see 'em. Layettes, pourin' in from all over. Can you imagine Roxie Hart a mother? That's like making Leopold and Loeb Scout Masters. (VELMA *pulls a chair over to* BILLY. *The Winch goes off with the* GIRLS *playing poker. Drum Doors close.*) Listen Billy, I figure if I am sensational in court, I could get things moving again, you know. I been thinkin' a lot about my trial. Could I just show you what I thought I might do on the witness stand?

BILLY. (*Disinterested.*) Yeah, sure . . . sure . . . go ahead.

(VELMA *signals cue to* ORCHESTRA. *Music starts. A* QUARTETTE, *all carrying megaphones, enters. The entire next musical number is choreographed around* VELMA *on and off the chair.*)

VELMA. Well, when I got on the stand, I thought I'd take a peek at the jury, and then I'd cross my legs like this, you know.

SONG: "WHEN VELMA TAKES THE STAND"

QUARTETTE. (*Sung.*)
WHEN VELMA TAKES THE STAND
VELMA. Then, when Harrison cross examines me, I thought

I'd give 'em this . . . and then if he yells at me I thought
I'd tremble like this . . .

QUARTETTE. (*Sung.*)
WHEN VELMA TAKES THE STAND

LOOK AT LITTLE VEL
SEE HER GIVE'EM HELL
AIN'T SHE DOIN' GRAND?
SHE'S GOT 'EM EATING OUT OF THE
PALM OF HER HAND!

VELMA. Then, I thought I'd let it all be too much for me,
like real dramatic. (*She makes a real dramatic gesture.*) Then,
I thought I'd get real thirsty and say, "Please, someone, could
I have a glass of water?"

QUARTETTE. (*Sung.*)
WHEN VELMA TAKES THE STAND

SEE THAT KELLY GIRL
MAKE THAT JURY WHIRL
WHEN SHE TURNS IT ON
SHE'S GONNA GET'EM GOIN'
'TILL SHE'S GOT'EM GONE

(ROXIE *enters and watches* VELMA *in the background* S. R.)

VELMA. Then, I thought I'd cry. Buckets. Only I don't have
a handkerchief—that's when I have to ask you for yours!
I really like that. Don't you? Then, I get up and try to walk,
only I'm too weak, and I slump and I slump and finally, I
faint! (*She faints.*)

QUARTETTE. (*Sung.*)
WHEN SHE ROLLS HER EYES
WATCH HER TAKE THE PRIZE

WHEN VELMA TAKES THE STAND!

(*She finishes, collapses over chair.* BOYS *exit. Now,* VELMA
raises her head.)

VELMA. How'd you like it?
BILLY. I like it. I like it.

ROXIE. Velma! Velma! Is that really what you're gonna do on the witness stand?

VELMA. Yeah. I thought so.

ROXIE. Can I offer you just the teeniest bit of criticism?

VELMA. Oh, okay!

ROXIE. It stinks!

BILLY. (*To* VELMA.) I'll talk to you later.

VELMA. I'm not hurt. I guess I'll go now. But not quietly. (*To the* ORCHESTRA.) May I have my exit music, please? (*The* ORCHESTRA *plays a vaudeville exit.* BOYS *re-enter.* VELMA *dances off with them.*)

QUARTETTE. (*Sung.*)
WHEN THEY SEE HER SHAKE
BET SHE TAKES THE CAKE
WHEN VELMA TAKES THE STAND

(QUARTETTE *dances off.*)

BILLY. (*Tough, to* ROXIE.) I've been waiting for you for ten minutes. Don't do that again. Okay, I got Amos to file for divorce.

ROXIE. (*Slightly arrogant.*) Yeah? So now what?

BILLY. So now I can get him on the stand and get him to admit that he made a terrible mistake because he still loves you. And of course, you still love him, and now the jury will be falling all over themselves to play cupid and get you back together again. Smart huh?

ROXIE. Smart huh.

BILLY. And another thing . . .

ROXIE. And another thing . . .

BILLY. When Amos is on the stand, I want you to be knitting.

ROXIE. *Knitting,* f'rchrissakes.

BILLY. A baby garment.

ROXIE. I don't know how to knit.

BILLY. Well, learn.

ROXIE. I don't wanna.

BILLY. I don't care what you don't wanna. It'll look good.

ROXIE. That's no way to get a jury's sympathy.

BILLY. Oh, now you don't need any advice right?

ROXIE. Seems to me Mr. Mouthpiece, that I come up with all the good ideas around here! (*A street fighter—tough.*) I am sick of everybody tellin' me what to do. Ya treat me like dirt, Billy Flynn. You treat me like some dumb, common criminal.

BILLY. But you *are* some dumb, common criminal.

ROXIE. (*Yelling.*) That's better than bein' a greasy Mick lawyer!

BILLY. (*Yelling back.*) Who happens to be saving your ass!

ROXIE. Who's out for all he can steal!

BILLY. You're getting a little too big for your bloomers, if you ask me.

ROXIE. Yeah, who asked you?

BILLY. Oh, maybe you could appear in court without me, too. Huh?

ROXIE. Maybe I could . . . just read the morning papers, palsie. They love me.

BILLY. Wise up, Kid. They'd love you a lot more if you were hanged. You know why? Because it would sell more papers.

ROXIE. You're fired!

BILLY. I quit! (*He starts out.*)

ROXIE. Any lawyer in this town would die to have my case!

BILLY. (*Stopping.*) You're a phony celebrity, kid. You're a flash-in-the-pan. In a couple of weeks, nobody'll even know who you are. That's Chicago. (*He leaves.*)

ROXIE. Oh, yeah?

BILLY. (*Calling back.*) Yeah! (*He goes up the* S. L. *stairs.* ROXIE *crosses to the pit as Drum Door opens and the Center Winch comes in.*)

ROXIE. (*Yelling after him.*) Yeah? We'll just see about that!

HUNYAK. (*In the dark as the Winch moves on.*) No. No. No.

(ROXIE *walks down the stairs to the pit.*)

ROXIE. (*Over her shoulder.*) And I want my five grand back, too!

HUNYAK. No. No. No.

(*Lights go out on* ROXIE, *as the lights come up on the Center Winch.*)

SCENE 4

SCENE: *An anteroom in the courthouse.*

AT RISE: HUNYAK *is being interrogated by her* LAWYER
(AARON) *and the* MATRON *is acting as her interpreter
with a Hungarian-English Dictionary in hand. The Scene
obviously has been going on for some time. It is also
obvious that* AARON *is impatient with his client's stub-
borness and her inability to speak "American."*

MATRON. (*To* AARON.) I'm sorry, Aaron. She still says
"No."

AARON. That much Hungarian I can understand. Ask her
once more.

MATRON. (*To* HUNYAK.) As ügyved szerint jobb ha bünösnék
vallja magát.

HUNYAK. Uh uh.

MATRON. She says "No."

AARON. (*Overlapping* MATRON's *line.*) I can understand *that,*
too! Jesus Christ, don't she know she's a loser for sure? Look,
tell her she's got no case. Tell her she'll be convicted! She'll
sit in jail. For *years.* How would she like that?

HUNYAK. Uncle Sam jò és igazsagos, ö nem fog börtönbe
csukni, mert artatlan vagyok.

AARON. Huh?

MATRON. Listen, you ought to get this accurately. She says
Uncle Sam is just and fair and he wouldn't put her in jail because she is innocent. Aaron, I think she's telling the truth.

AARON. So what? What the hell has innocence got to do with
it? Look, Mrs. Morton, this is a court appointed thing, you
know? I don't get anything from this, understand. Nothing
at all!

MATRON. Whaddya want from me? I've done my best.

HUNYAK. (*With great difficulty.*) Not . . . guil . . . ty.

AARON. Goddam foreign hunky nut.

HUNYAK. Fogok tetszeni Uncle Sam-nek?

AARON. Huh?

MATRON. She says will Uncle Sam like her?

AARON. I don't give a Goddamn what she says unless it's
"guilty."

HUNYAK. Not . . . guil . . . ty.

(BAILIFF *enters* s. l.)

BAILIFF. Aaron?
AARON. Yes.
BAILIFF. He's ready for you.
MATRON. (*To* HUNYAK.) Well, here you go.

(*Music up.* AARON *and the* BAILIFF *exit.* HUNYAK *walks toward the audience and bows.*)

HUNYAK. Not guil . . . ty. Not guil . . . ty. Not guilty Uncle Sam. (*She walks Upstage to a rope ladder that has been flown in* s. l. *and removes her prison garment to reveal a circus costume. She climbs up the rope ladder. Backing off stage the* MATRON *announces a la Circus Ring Master style:*)
MATRON. And now, ladies and gentlemen, for your pleasure and your entertainment—we proudly present . . . the one . . . the only Katalin Hunyak and her famous Hungarian rope trick.

(HUNYAK *disappears off stage. Drum roll, crescendo, cymbal crash. Sound of a crowd. Behind a screen in the Center drum, we see a silhouette of a* WOMAN *hanging from a rope. On both sides, we see two pairs of hands applauding in slow motion. Sound of newspaper City Room.*)

ANNOUNCER. (*Off Stage.*) After 47 years a Cook County precedent has been shattered. Katalin Hunyak was hanged tonight for the brutal axe murder of her husband. The Hungarian woman's last words were, "Not guilty."

(*Lights dim out on silhouette and come up on anteroom.* BILLY *enters the anteroom from* s. r. *and* ROXIE *comes up the stairs from the pit.*)

SCENE 5

SCENE: *The anteroom of the courthouse, March 9th.*

AT RISE: ROXIE *is dressed in a dress with lace around the neck and on the cuffs of her sleeves. She enters pulling at the lace.* BILLY *is rummaging through some papers in his briefcase.*

ROXIE. Billy . . . Billy, *I hate this dress!*

BILLY. It's what I want you to wear.

ROXIE. I look like a Woolworth's lamp shade. I don't wanna wear it.

BILLY. You're wearin' whatever I tell you to wear. As a matter of fact, you're *doin'* whatever I tell you to *do*. That was the deal, remember?

ROXIE. I don't remember nothin' about a dress.

BILLY. No? "Please, Billy," you said. "Come back. I need you, Billy." Right after they hanged the Hunyak? You remember that, don't ya? Yeah, you said . . . "I'm sorry. I'm scared. I'll do anything you say." Did ya say that or didn't ya?

ROXIE. Maybe I did.

BILLY. So shut up about the dress. Now we're clear about everything you're going to do on the stand, right?

ROXIE. Don't worry about me. I been up all night rehearsing. I know every line.

BILLY. Alright, let's get to my summation. Now, I'm gonna start with justice and America—blah-blah-blah—then I'll get to your repentence—blah-blah-blah—then I'll say, "If sorrow could avail, Fred Casely would be here now, for she would give her life and gladly, to bring the dead man back." You nod.

ROXIE. That's all?

BILLY. That's all! Then I say— "But we can't do that, gentlemen. You may take her life as the State demands, but it won't bring Casely back." That's always news to them. And then I go into my final statement, winding up . . . "We can't give her happiness. But we *can* give her another chance." And that's all for you.

ROXIE. All for me?

BILLY. That's it.

ROXIE. Like hell it is. It's me they want to see! Not you.

BILLY. It's my speech that brings 'em in and it's my speech that'll save your neck.

ROXIE. (*Pulling lace up over her nose.*) If they can see it through all this crappy lace.

BILLY. (*They are back at it again.*) Look, I'm running this!

ROXIE. Screw you, you Goddamned old crook!

BILLY. (*Overlapping* ROXIE's *line.*) Shut up, you dirty little— (*Door opens,* BAILIFF *enters.*)

BAILIFF. Mr. Flynn, his honor is here.

BILLY. (*Quietly.*) Thank you. Just a moment. (*The* BAILIFF *exits.* ROXIE *rushes Down Stage Center. She mimes looking into a mirror.*) You ready?

ROXIE. (*Nervously.*) Yeah, I'm ready. (*VAMP under.*)

BILLY. (*Gentle for the first time.*) Hey, don't be scared, Roxie. It'll be all right. I've been around a long time, and believe me, you got nothin' to worry about.

ROXIE. (*Nervously.*) Yeah, nothing to worry about. Oh Billy, I am worried. (*She goes off* S. L. BILLY *gets ready for his courtroom "scene"—pulling his shirt out, roughing up his hair, exposing some down-home suspenders—his "Clarence Darrow" look.*)

BILLY. (*To the audience.*) It's all a circus, Kid. A three ring circus. These trials—the whole world—all show business. But kid, you're working with a star, the biggest! (*VAMP up strong.*)

SONG: "RAZZLE DAZZLE"

(*Sung:*)
GIVE'EM THE OLD RAZZLE DAZZLE
RAZZLE DAZZLE 'EM

(*A* DANCER *starts to enter.*)

GIVE'EM AN ACT WITH LOTS OF FLASH IN IT
AND THE REACTION WILL BE PASSIONATE

(*Another* DANCER *enters.*)

GIVE'EM THE OLD HOCUS POCUS
BEAD AND FEATHER 'EM
HOW CAN THEY SEE WITH SEQUINS IN THEIR
    EYES?

WHAT IF YOUR HINGES ALL ARE RUSTING?
WHAT IF, IN FACT, YOU'RE JUST DISGUSTING?

RAZZLE DAZZLE 'EM
AND THEY'LL NEVER CATCH WISE!

(*Entire* Company *is now on stage; they dance in slow motion.*)

GIVE 'EM THE OLD RAZZLE DAZZLE
   Billy and Company.
RAZZLE DAZZLE 'EM
GIVE 'EM A SHOW THAT'S SO SPLENDIFEROUS
   Billy.
ROW AFTER ROW WILL GROW VOCIFEROUS
   Billy and Company.
GIVE 'EM THE OLD FLIM FLAM FLUMMOX
FOOL AND FRACTURE 'EM
   Billy.
HOW CAN THEY HEAR THE TRUTH ABOVE THE
   ROAR?
   Billy and Company.
THROW'EM A FAKE AND A FINAGLE
THEY'LL NEVER KNOW, YOU'RE JUST A BAGEL,
   Billy.
RAZZLE DAZZLE'EM
   Billy and Company.
AND THEY'LL BEG YOU FOR MORE!
   (*As the* Company *dances, the set begins to change for the*
   Courtroom.)
GIVE'EM THE OLD RAZZLE DAZZLE
RAZZLE DAZZLE 'EM

BACK SINCE THE DAYS OF OLD METHUSALEH
EVERYONE LOVES THE BIG BAMBOOZ-A-LER
   (Billy *walks up the back steps to the Bandstand and*
   finishes the number from there.)
GIVE'EM THE OLD THREE RING CIRCUS
STUN AND STAGGER'EM

WHEN YOU'RE IN TROUBLE, GO INTO YOUR
   DANCE
THOUGH YOU ARE STIFFER THAN A GIRDER
THEY LET YA GET AWAY WITH MURDER

RAZZLE DAZZLE 'EM
AND YOU'VE GOT A ROMANCE

BILLY. (*Juggles as he sings.*)

GIVE 'EM THE OLD RAZZLE DAZZLE

RAZZLE DAZZLE 'EM

COMPANY.

GIVE 'EM THE OLD RAZZLE DAZZLE

BILLY and COMPANY.

GIVE'EM AN ACT THAT'S UNASSAILABLE

THEY'LL WAIT A YEAR 'TIL YOU'RE AVAILABLE!

BILLY.

GIVE 'EM THE OLD DOUBLE WHAMMY

DAZE AND DIZZY 'EM

COMPANY.

GIVE 'EM THE OLD DOUBLE WHAMMY

BILLY.

SHOW'EM THE FIRST RATE SORCERER YOU ARE

BILLY and COMPANY.

LONG AS YOU KEEP 'EM WAY OFF BALANCE

HOW CAN THEY SPOT YOU GOT NO TALENTS?

BILLY.

RAZZLE DAZZLE 'EM

COMPANY.

RAZZLE DAZZLE 'EM

BILLY.

RAZZLE DAZZLE 'EM

BILLY and COMPANY.

AND THEY'LL MAKE YOU A STAR!

(*The* COMPANY *crosses to form a group Center Stage as number ends. Music segues after applause.*)

SCENE 6

SCENE: *The Courtroom.*

AT RISE: *The* COMPANY, *standing Center Stage, introduces the scene:*

COMPANY. Ladies and gentlemen, we present—Justice. The State of Illinois versus Roxie Hart for the murder of Fred Casely. Thank you. (*As the* COMPANY *moves in slow motion to their places on the stairs, a Winch comes in* S. L. *with 12 chairs representing the Jury box. One* ACTOR, *in various dis-*

guises, which he changes throughout the Scene is ostensibly
all 12 people on the Jury. ROXIE *enters* S. L. *She sits and knits.*
BILLY *comes down the stairs, and enters the action.*) The
State calls Mr. Amos Hart. (*As the stage clears, we see* AMOS
being sworn in by the CLERK.)

CLERK. Blah, blah, blah, blah, blah, blah . . . truth . . .
truth . . . truth. Selp-you God.

AMOS. I certainly do. (CLERK *exits.*)

HARRISON. (*From a typewritten paper.*) "Question by Sergeant Fogarty: "What happened next?" Answer by Roxie
Hart: "I shot him, because he was walking out on me, the
louse." (*Music out. Very dramatically.*) Signed Roxie Hart.
(*Hands paper to* AMOS.) Do you recognize the signature?

AMOS. (*Looking at the paper.*) Yes sir, it's the signature of
the lady who used to be my wife.

HARRISON. Exactly. Take the witness. (BILLY *rises and*
crosses to AMOS. *Music under.*)

BILLY. Hello, Amos.

AMOS. (*Amazed that* BILLY *got his name right.*) Amos, that's
right, Mr. Flynn. Amos.

BILLY. (*Very pleasantly.*) Amos, you are at present obtaining
a divorce from the defendant?

AMOS. Yes, sir.

BILLY. When did you file suit?

AMOS. A few weeks ago.

BILLY. Was there any reason for your filing for divorce at
this particular time?

AMOS. I'll say! The newspapers said that she was expecting
a little stranger.

BILLY. (*Super charming.*) Well, that's hardly grounds for
divorce, is it?

AMOS. A little too *much* of a stranger.

BILLY. Oh, by that you mean you doubted the paternity of
the child.

AMOS. (*Narrow-eyed, at* BILLY.) Well, sure!

BILLY. (*Losing his friendliness.*) Did you question her after
you read it? Did you even bother to ask her if you were the
father?

AMOS. No sir, but you told me . . .

BILLY. (*Quickly, interrupting.*) Just jumped to a conclusion?
Do you call that playing square? Let me ask you this, Hart—

if you became convinced you were wrong—you'd be man enough to admit it, wouldn't ya? You'd even be willing to take her back, wouldn't ya? If Roxie Hart *swore* that you were the father of her child, which she does . . .

AMOS. She does?

ROXIE. I do.

BILLY. She does. Step down, Daddy. (*Hands* AMOS *a cigar. Back to being charming:*) The defense calls Roxie Hart.

CLERK. Roxie Hart to the stand. (ROXIE *crosses to the stand as a bewildered* AMOS *rises.* ROXIE *stops before* AMOS, *kisses him on the cheek and hands him her knitting.* AMOS *walks dazedly off.* ROXIE *takes the stand. The* CLERK *holds a Bible in front of her.*) Blah, blah, blah, blah, blah, blah, . . . truth . . . truth . . . truth. Selp-yuh God.

ROXIE. I do.

BILLY. (*Approaching her.*) What is your name?

ROXIE. Roxie Hart.

BILLY. Roxie, I have here a statement in which you admit having had illicit relations with the deceased, Fred Casely. Is this statement true or false?

ROXIE. I'm afraid that's true.

BILLY. You're an honest girl, Roxie. When did you first meet Fred Casely?

ROXIE. (*Well-rehearsed.*) When he sold Amos and me our furniture. Also he was a regular patron at the nightclub where I was a member of the chorus.

BILLY. And your personal relationship with him—could you tell the jury—when did that begin?

ROXIE. When I permitted him to drive me home one night.

(FRED *enters. Charleston beat begins. He dances through the following.*)

FRED. Hey, chickie.

ROXIE. (*To the audience.*) Hello, Mr. Casely.

FRED. Fine night for ducks, ain't it? I got my car right around the corner. Why don't I drive you home? It's raining so hard and all.

COMPANY. Charleston, Charleston . . . (*Winds down.*) Charleston. (FRED *exits dancing.*)

ROXIE. (*Softly.*) Oh, he seemed like such a fine gentleman, and he dressed so elegantly.

BILLY. Yet, you were married, Mrs. Hart.

ROXIE. I know. And I don't think I would have gone with him if Mr. Hart and me hadn't quarreled that very morning.

BILLY. Quarreled?

ROXIE. (*Drops her head.*) Yes, sir.

BILLY. I suppose it was his fault.

ROXIE. Oh, no, sir. It was my fault. Seems I just couldn't stop pesterin' him. (AMOS *enters with a newspaper.*)

BILLY. Pesterin' him? About what?

ROXIE. (*To* AMOS, *who is standing beside her, reading a newspaper.*) Oh, Amos, I don't want to work in that cheap Southside nightclub. I don't like you working those long hours at the garage either. Oh Amos, I want you home with me. I want to do your laundry. I want to darn your socks. I want to iron your shirts. I want a real home and a child. (*Music out.*)

BILLY. So . . . you drifted into this illicit relationship with Fred Casely because you were unhappy at home.

ROXIE. *Most* unhappy.

AMOS. (*Twisting* ROXIE's *"boob."*) I love ya, honey. I love ya.

BILLY. Yet, you do respect the sacredness of the marriage vow?

ROXIE. Oh yes, sir.

BILLY. Then why did you continue in this affair with Casely. Why didn't you stop?

ROXIE. I did *want* to! I *tried* to. But Mr. Casely, he'd plead and he'd . . . (FRED *enters again.*) say . . .

FRED. (*Grabbing her, bouncing her up and down on the stand.*) I can't live without you! I can't live without you! I can't live without you! (FRED *exits.*)

AMOS. (*Grabbing her "boob" immediately.*) I love ya, honey. I love ya. (AMOS *exits.*)

ROXIE. I was being torn apart.

BILLY. (*Super dramatic.*) Roxie Hart, the State has accused you of the murder of Fred Casely. Are you guilty or not guilty?

ROXIE. Not guilty! Not guilty! Oh, I killed him—yes—but I'm not a criminal!

BILLY. (*Handing* ROXIE *a handkerchief.*) There, there . . . (ROXIE *remembers to sob.* COMPANY *begins the "Methusaleh" chorus of "RAZZLE DAZZLE" softly underneath the following:*) Roxie, can you recall the night of February 14th?

ROXIE. Yes sir.

BILLY. Tell the Jury, in your own way, the happenings of that night.

ROXIE. (*Leaving the stand during the following to act it out.*) Well, it was after work about 2 a.m. and I stopped in at an all night grocery store to pick up some baking powder to make cup cakes for my Amos. Oh Amos just loved my cup cakes. And then, I went right home. And I took my bath and I was getting ready for bed when, suddenly the doorbell rang. (*We hear door bell, and a door rolls on* S. R. *Music out.* ROXIE *takes off dress and crosses to the door.*) Now, I thought it was my friend, Gloria, so I slipped into my kimona and went to the door. (*She puts on her kimona.* ROXIE *opens the door to* FRED, *who stands behind the door.*)

BILLY. And who was there? (*Chord.*)

ROXIE. Fred Casely. (*Music up.*)

BILLY. And what did he say, Roxie?

FRED. Hello, Roxie. I had to see you once more.

ROXIE. Why, Fred?

FRED. That note you wrote me. Telling me it was all over? Telling me we had to quit? Saying it could never end in happiness? Why did you write that note, Roxie?

ROXIE. Because I have reformed. (*Music out.*) Because I have seen the error of my ways and oh . . . and oh . . . (*Looks for help.*)

BILLY. And did he go away as you asked him to?

HARRISON. I object to Counsel's leading the witness.

JUDGE. Sustained.

BILLY. I'll rephrase the question. And what did you say?

ROXIE. Oh! . . . Go away! (CHORUS *applauds.* BILLY *and* ROXIE *acknowledge it.* FRED *and* ROXIE *then act out the following.*) I tried to close the door, but he forced his way in. I ran into the bedroom, but he followed me. (*Door off.* FRED *follows* ROXIE *across the stage. She stops.*)

BILLY. And then?

FRED. Look, just have one little drink with me and I'll go.

BILLY. (*To* ROXIE.) Why didn't you scream?

ROXIE. I was afraid of waking up the neighbors. (*To* FRED *in a stage whisper.*) Please, no good will come of this, and besides, I love my husband. (ROXIE *falls to her knees.*)

COMPANY.

HALLELUJAH! HALLELUJAH! HALLELUJAH!

BILLY. So . . . you told him that you loved your husband and what did he say to that?

FRED. It doesn't matter. You're mine. You're mine. You're mine. (*He shakes her. Apache music begins. He flings her aside. She falls over the witness stand.*)

ROXIE. I can't go on. I can't. I can't.

BILLY. No, no. No, Roxie, you must tell the Jury everything. They have a right to know. (ROXIE *rises, walks back to* FRED *and taps him on the shoulder.*)

ROXIE. Amos and me are going to have a baby.

BILLY. And what did he say to that?

FRED. I'll kill you before I see you have another man's child! (FRED *lunges at* ROXIE. *They freeze.*)

BILLY. Diagram! (*Drum roll.* MAN *enters* S. L. *with diagram of the Hart Apartment.*) Where were you at this time? (ROXIE *walks* U. S., *with a wiggle, to the diagram.*)

ROXIE. (*Seductively to the Jury—pointing to diagram.*) I was by the victrola.

BILLY. And where was Casely? Show the Jury.

ROXIE. (*Pointing to diagram.*) He was also by the victrola.

BILLY. Show the Jury what happened next.

ROXIE. In his passion he ripped off my kimona and threw me on the bed . . . (*She takes off kimona and flings it over the diagram. She and* FRED *act out the following:*) Mr. Hart's revolver was layin' there between us. He grabbed for the gun— I knocked it from his hand—he whirled me aside.

BILLY. And then?

ROXIE. And then, we both reached for the gun. (*Chord.*) But I got it first.

COMPANY. Hurray!

ROXIE. Then, he came toward me with this funny look in his eyes.

BILLY. What kind of look?

ROXIE. I dunno. Angry. Wild!

FRED. I mean to kill you!

BILLY. Did you think he meant to kill you?

ROXIE. (*Staring at* FRED, *but talking to* BILLY.) Oh, yes, sir. (*She backs up.* FRED *comes toward her.* BILLY *steps in between them.*)

BILLY. Then, it was his life or yours?

ROXIE. (*Goes to Jury, pats her stomach.*) And not just mine! (*Back to* FRED.) And I closed my eyes and shot . . .

COMPANY. (*Hits tambourines three times.*) Hey! (FRED *falls —dead.*)

BILLY. In defense of your life?

COMPANY. (*Sung.*)

RAZZLE DAZZLE 'EM

ROXIE. To save my hus-   COMPANY. (*Sung.*)
band's innocent unborn child!   RAZZLE DAZZLE 'EM

COMPANY. (*Sung.*)

AND THEY'LL MAKE YOU A STAR

(*The* COMPANY, ROXIE *and* BILLY *bow.*)

BLACKOUT

SCENE 7

SCENE: *A room in the Jail.*

AT RISE: VELMA *and the* MATRON *ride up on the* S. R. *elevator. They are seated at a table with a radio between them. The* MATRON *listens intently.* VELMA *plays with a deck of cards.* MARY SUNSHINE *speaks into a microphone on the Bandstand. During the scene, her voice seems to be coming out of the radio on the table.*

MARY SUNSHINE. Mrs. Hart's behavior throughout this ordeal has been truly extraordinary . . .

VELMA. (*Sarcastically, over* SUNSHINE'S *commentary.*) I bet it has.

MARY SUNSHINE. Seated next to her attorney, Mr. Billy Flynn, she weeps . . . (VELMA *laughs.*) . . . but she fishes in her handbag and cannot find a handkerchief . . .

VELMA. Handkerchief?

MARY SUNSHINE. . . . Finally, her attorney, Mr. Flynn, hands her one . . .

VELMA. That's *my* bit.

MATRON. (*Shushing her.*) Shhh . . . I wanna hear.

MARY SUNSHINE. The poor child has had no relief. She looks around now, bewildered, seeming to want something. Oh, it's a glass of water. The bailiff has brought her one.

VELMA. A glass of water! That's mine too!

MARY SUNSHINE. Mrs. Hart, her usual gracious self, thanks

the bailiff and he smiles at her. She looks simply radiant in
her stylish blue lace dress and elegant silver shoes.

VELMA. (*To the Radio.*) With rhinestone buckles?

MARY SUNSHINE. With rhinestone buckles. (*Lights fade out
on* MARY SUNSHINE *as she exits.* VELMA *clicks off the radio
and picks it up getting ready to throw it.* MATRON *stops her.*)

MATRON. Velma, don't break my radio!

VELMA. (*Upset.*) But those were my shoes and she stole
'em!

MATRON. Well, you shouldn't have left them layin' around.

VELMA. First she steals my publicity, my lawyer, my trial
date, and now, my shoes.

MATRON. Well, whaddya expect? She's a low brow. The whole
world's gone low brow. Things ain't what they used to be.
(*Music up.*)

VELMA. They sure ain't. It's all gone.

SONG: "CLASS"

VELMA. (*Sung.*)
WHATEVER HAPPENED TO FAIR DEALING?
AND PURE ETHICS
AND NICE MANNERS?
WHY IS IT EVERYONE NOW
    IS A PAIN IN THE ASS?
WHATEVER HAPPENED TO CLASS?
    MATRON. (*Sung.*)
CLASS.
WHATEVER HAPPENED TO, "PLEASE, MAY I?"
AND, "YES, THANK YOU"?
AND, "HOW CHARMING"?
NOW, EVERY SON OF A BITCH
    IS A SNAKE IN THE GRASS
WHATEVER HAPPENED TO CLASS?
    VELMA and MATRON.
CLASS!

AH, THERE AIN'T NO GENTLEMEN
    TO OPEN UP THE DOORS
THERE AIN'T NO LADIES NOW,
    THERE'S ONLY PIGS AND WHORES
AND EVEN KIDS'D KNOCK YA DOWN
    SO'S THEY CAN PASS

NOBODY'S GOT NO CLASS!
VELMA.
WHATEVER HAPPENED TO OLD VALUES?
MATRON.
AND FINE MORALS?
VELMA.
AND GOOD BREEDING?
MATRON.
NOW, NO ONE EVEN SAYS "OOPS"
    WHEN THEY'RE PASSING THEIR GAS
VELMA and MATRON.
WHATEVER HAPPENED TO CLASS?

CLASS
VELMA and MATRON.
AH, THERE AIN'T NO GENTLEMEN
    THAT'S FIT FOR ANY USE
AND ANY GIRL'D TOUCH YOUR PRIVATES
    FOR A DEUCE
MATRON.
AND EVEN KIDS'LL KICK YOUR SHINS
    AND GIVE YOU SASS
VELMA. (*A beat behind.*)
AND EVEN KIDS'LL KICK YOUR SHINS
    AND GIVE YOU SASS
VELMA and MATRON.
NOBODY'S GOT NO CLASS!

(ORCHESTRA *up, lushly played.*)

VELMA. (*Over.*)
ALL YOU READ ABOUT TODAY IS RAPE AND
    THEFT
MATRON.
JESUS CHRIST, AIN'T THERE NO DECENCY LEFT?
VELMA and MATRON.
NOBODY'S GOT NO CLASS
MATRON.
EVERYBODY YOU WATCH
VELMA.
'S GOT HIS BRAINS IN HIS CROTCH
MATRON.
HOLY CRAP

VELMA.
HOLY CRAP
MATRON.
WHAT A SHAME
VELMA.
WHAT A SHAME
VELMA and MATRON.
WHAT BECAME OF CLASS?

(*Elevator sinks slowly on last note.*)

LIGHTS FADE OUT

SCENE 8

SCENE: *The Courtroom.*

AT RISE: MARY SUNSHINE *is seated at a small table* S. R. BILLY
  FLYNN *enters and crosses Center, to stand with his back
  to the audience. Drum roll.*

MARY SUNSHINE. (*Into microphone.*) Ladies and gentlemen,
the final day of the trial of Roxie Hart has come. A hush has
fallen over the courtroom as Mr. Billy Flynn prepares his
summation to the jury. The next voice you hear will be that of
Mr. Flynn, champion of the down-trodden. (*A* LADY *representing Justice enters and takes a place on the stairs,* S. R. *She
holds a sword and the scales of Justice. A* MAN *representing
Uncle Sam enters and takes a place on the stairs* S. L. *He holds
an American flag.*)
  BILLY. (*Music under. Turning to the audience. Sincerely.*)
Ladies and gentlemen, you and I have never killed. We can't
know the agony, the hell that Roxie Hart lived through then.
This drunken beast, Fred Casely, forced his way into her
home, forced liquor upon her, physically abused her and
threatened her life. At that moment, mother love and a deep
concern for her neighbors stirred within her. She shot him.
We don't deny that. But she has prayed to God for forgive-
ness for what she has done. Yes, you may take her life, but
it won't bring Casely back. (ROXIE *enters, stands under the
flag.*) Look, look closely at that frail figure. My God, hasn't

she been punished enough? We can't give her happiness, but we can give her another chance. You have heard my colleague call her temptress, call her adultress, call her murderess. But, despite what the Prosecution says, things are not always what they appear to be. (BILLY *crosses to* MARY SUNSHINE. *Circus-ey music plays as* MARY SUNSHINE *sings a coloratura trill.* BILLY *removes her wig and dress to reveal her to be a him in his boxer shorts. They bow to each other.*) The defense rests! (*He,* MARY SUNSHINE, *exits.*)

LIGHTS FADE

SCENE 9

SCENE: *The Courtroom.*

AT RISE: *The same as Scene 8, except* THREE REPORTERS *have come in to the Courtroom to hear the verdict. Music under.* BILLY *crosses to* ROXIE.

JUDGE. Gentlemen of the Jury. Have you reached a verdict?
FOREMAN. We have, your Honor.
JUDGE. Will the defendant please rise? (*Music fades.*) And what is your verdict?
FOREMAN. We find the defendant . . . (*Gun shots and a scream Off Stage cover the* FOREMAN's *announcement of the verdict. Enormous confusion and shouting in the wings.— A* REPORTER *rushes in.*)
REPORTER. (*Excited.*) You should see what's going on out there! There was this divorce action and this babe shot her husband, his mother, and the defense attorney. There is blood all over the walls. It's terrible. It's awful. But what a story! (*The stage clears quickly except for* BILLY *and* ROXIE.)
ROXIE. (*Running after the* REPORTERS.) I'm Roxie Hart! I'm Roxie Hart! Don't you want my picture? I'm the famous Roxie. What's goin' on around here? What the hell happened? (*Crossing back to* BILLY.)
BILLY. You were found not guilty, that's what happened.
ROXIE. Who the hell cares about that?
BILLY. I saved your life.

ROXIE. Where are all the photographers—the reporters? The publicity? My name in the papers. I was countin' on that. I was countin' on that.

BILLY. You know, your gratitude is overwhelming. But forget it, I'm only in it for the money anyway.

ROXIE. Yeah, you get five thousand dollars and I wind up with nothin'.

BILLY. You're a free woman, Roxie Hart, and God save Illinois. Well, I guess that finishes us, Roxie. (*To the audience.*) And that's the last *you'll* see of me, too. (*To the Bandstand.*) My exit music please. (*We hear the strains of* "ALL I CARE ABOUT." *The* FAN DANCERS *enter to escort* BILLY *off.*)

BILLY and FAN DANCERS. (*Sung.*)
ALL I (HE) CARE(S) ABOUT IS LOVE

(*They walk off.* AMOS *enters, crosses to* ROXIE.)

AMOS. Roxie?

ROXIE. What do you want?

AMOS. I'd like you to come home. You said you still wanted me. I still love *you.* And the baby. Our baby . . .

ROXIE. Baby? What baby? Jesus, what do you take me for? There ain't no baby!

AMOS. There ain't no baby?

ROXIE. That's right.

AMOS. (*Long beat.*) Roxie, I still love you.

ROXIE. (*Ignores him—sadly to herself.*) They didn't even want my picture. I don't understand that. They didn't even want my picture.

AMOS. (*Starts to exit. Calls up to Bandstand.*) My exit music, please . . . (*The* ORCHESTRA *doesn't play.*) . . . Okay. (AMOS *shrugs and shuffles off like Bert Williams.*)

ROXIE. (*Speaks to no one in particular.*) . . . gone . . .

SONG: "NOWADAYS"

(*Sung.*)
IT'S GOOD, ISN'T IT?

GRAND, ISN'T IT?
GREAT, ISN'T IT?
SWELL, ISN'T IT?
FUN, ISN'T IT?
NOWADAYS

THERE'S MEN, EVERYWHERE
JAZZ, EVERYWHERE
BOOZE, EVERYWHERE
LIFE, EVERYWHERE
JOY, EVERYWHERE
NOWADAYS

YOU CAN LIKE THE LIFE YOU'RE LIVING
YOU CAN LIVE THE LIFE YOU LIKE
YOU CAN EVEN MARRY HARRY
BUT MESS AROUND WITH IKE
AND THAT'S

GOOD, ISN'T IT?
GRAND, ISN'T IT?
GREAT, ISN'T IT?
SWELL, ISN'T IT?
FUN, ISN'T IT . . .
        (*Going off.*)

(*Music swells as* ROXIE *walks off. The set begins to change,
the music swells. We hear a* MASTER OF CEREMONIES *speaking from the Bandstand.*)

MASTER OF CEREMONIES. Ladies and gentlemen, the Vickers
Theatre, Chicago's finest home of family entertainment, is
proud to announce a first. The first time, anywhere, there has
been an act of this nature. Not only one little lady, but two!
You've read about them in the papers and now here they are—
a double header! Chicago's own killer dillers—those two
scintillating sinners—Roxie Hart and Velma Kelly. (*Drum
Doors open. We see* ROXIE *and* VELMA *with top hats and canes.
Fade out on* M.C. ROXIE *and* VELMA *walk forward. Drum
Doors close.*)

SONG: "NOWADAYS"/"R.S.V.P."/"KEEP IT HOT"

Roxie and Velma. (*Sung.*)
YOU CAN LIKE THE LIFE YOU'RE LIVING
YOU CAN LIVE THE LIFE YOU LIKE
YOU CAN EVEN MARRY HARRY
BUT MESS AROUND WITH IKE
AND THAT'S

GOOD, ISN'T IT?
GRAND, ISN'T IT?
GREAT, ISN'T IT?
SWELL, ISN'T IT?
FUN, ISN'T IT?
BUT NOTHING STAYS

IN FIFTY YEARS OR SO
IT'S GONNA CHANGE, YOU KNOW
BUT, OH, IT'S HEAVEN
NOWADAYS

(*Music continues.* Bandleader *whistles under as* M.C. *enters* s. r. *with microphone.*)

Master of Ceremonies. (*Into microphone* s. r.) And now, poetry in motion—two moving as one. (*He exits with microphone.* Roxie *and* Velma *dance, ending with:*)
Roxie and Velma. (*Sung.*)
WA, WA, WA, WA ETC. . . .
AND THAT'S
GOOD, ISN'T IT?
GRAND, ISN'T IT?
GREAT, ISN'T IT?
SWELL, ISN'T IT?
FUN, ISN'T IT?
BUT NOTHING STAYS

IN FIFTY YEARS OR SO
IT'S GONNA CHANGE, YOU KNOW
BUT, OH, IT'S HEAVEN
NOWADAYS.

(*Number finishes. The* M.C. *enters, again* S. R., *with microphone.*)

MASTER OF CEREMONIES. (*Into microphone.*) Okay, you babes of jazz. Let's pick up the pace. Let's shake the blues away. Let's make the parties longer. Let's make the skirts shorter and shorter. Let's make the music hotter. Let's all go to hell in a fast car and *KEEP IT HOT!* (*He exits with microphone.* ROXIE *and* VELMA *dance until their turn seems to have come to an end.* Two MEN *bring in bouquets of flowers, hand them to* ROXIE *and* VELMA, *then exit.* VELMA *puts her hand up to the audience for quiet. She addresses the audience as* ROXIE *stands, shyly, beside her.*)

VELMA. (*To the audience.*) Thank you. Roxie and I would just like to take this opportunity to thank you. Not only for the way you treated us tonight, but for before this—for your faith and your belief in our innocence.

ROXIE. It was your letters, telegrams, and words of encouragement that helped see us through our terrible ordeal. Believe us, we could not have done it without you. (*As* ORCHESTRA *plays the Battle Hymn of the Republic.*)

VELMA. You know, a lot of people have lost faith in America.

ROXIE. And for what America stands for.

VELMA. But we are the living examples of what a wonderful country this is. (*They hug and pose.*)

ROXIE. So we'd just like to say thank you and God Bless you.

VELMA and ROXIE. God Bless you. Thank you and God bless you. . . . God be with you. God walk with you always. God bless you. God bless you.

(*Music up. They stand, bowing, throwing roses to the audience, waving and smiling, as . . .*)

THE CURTAIN FALLS

COSTUME PLOT

Act One—
red suit with blue pinstripe (pants are break-away)
fleur de lis shirt
red tie
brocade vest
suit of underwear, boxer shorts
black shoes, socks, and garters
grey spats on shoes

Change: during song "All I Care About"
strips down to suit of underwear, shoes, socks, and garters

Change: during Scene 8 he dresses in
gold patterned suit
white shirt
vest
brown tie

Change: after song "We Both Reached For The Gun" he
changes back to
red suit with blue pinstripes
dark red vest

Act Two—
same as end of Act One

Change: after "Mr. Cellophane" for "Velma Takes The
Stand"
blue suit and vest with red pinstripe
blue shirt, white collar and cuffs
matching tie
handkerchief

Change: before "Razzle Dazzle"
jacket is struck
vest is struck onstage

Change: for "Bow"
blue suit, shirt, tie

Gwen Verdon as Roxie Hart

Act One—
  wig—blonde
  silver sequin dress, matching purse
  black shoes with silver strip
  black hose

  Change: when she enters her apartment (the drum)
  peach-colored satin teddies
  black hose

  Change: after song "All That Jazz" and dialogue
  black sequin dress (over teddies)
  black shoes with rhinestone heels
  feathered head band

  Change: after song "Funny Honey"
  black plastic striped net jail robe (over teddies)
  black ribbon head band
  black patent shoes

  Change: after "Tap Dance" into costume for "Roxy" under
      jail robe
  black bikini, strands of black bugle beads
  silver sequin shoes

  Change: onstage for "Roxy"
  strikes jail robe

  Change: after "Roxy"
  teddies
  floral robe
  black shoes

  Change: onstage for "My Own Best Friend"—strikes robe
  black trench coat
  creme-colored wide-brimmed hat

Act Two—for "Me and My Baby" strut version
  black tights
  black vest
  black bowler
  high-button black shoes with grey spats
  black choker

Change: after "Me And My Baby" strut
teddies
floral robe
black patent shoes with bows

Change: after Scene 3
lace dress (over teddies)
lace dickey
lace head band
silver shoes

Change: during Scene 6
strike dress, dickey, add
flowered robe

Change: end of Scene 6
white satin tank
lace dress, dickey, headband
bouquet of flowers

Change: after song "Nowadays"
strike lace dress, dickey, head band. Add
white tuxedo jacket with tails
white top hat
cane

Change: during "Act"
strike jacket, cane, hat. Add
beaded and sequined fringe skirt

CHITA RIVERA AS VELMA KELLY

Act One—
wig
tights
G string
black body stocking
black lace pants
black stockings, garters, red garter
black shoes
black fishnet dress with jewelled buckle
black feathered head band

Change: after "All That Jazz"
strikes red garter, head band, dress. Adds
black plastic striped net jail robe
black beaded head band

Change: after "Cell Block Tango"
strikes jail robe. Adds
flowered robe

Change: onstage for "My Own Best Friend"
strikes robe. Add
black trench coat
creme-colored wide-brimmed hat

Act Two—
black panties
red beaded top
black fringed skirt
red shoes
red beaded head band

Change: after "I Know A Girl"
strikes top, skirt, head band, shoes, pants. Adds
G string
black body stocking
black lace panties
black voile dress with rose patches
flowered robe
black shoes

Change: onstage for "Velma Takes The Stand"
strikes robe

Change: after "Velma Takes The Stand"
strikes dress, pants, G string, body stocking. Adds
white satin tank
flowered robe

Change: after "Class"
strikes flowered robe, shoes. Adds
white tuxedo jacket with tails

white top hat
cane

Change: during "Act"
strike jacket, cane, hat. Add
beaded and sequined fringe skirt

BARNEY MARTIN AS AMOS HART

Act One—
dirty tee shirt
dirty coveralls
work shoes

Change: after "Funny Honey"
clean tee shirt
brown slacks
striped dress shirt with white bib
sleeveless brown cardigan
cordovan oxfords
beige cap

Act Two—
striped dress shirt
cardigan
baggy black pants
red clown shoes
cap

Change: onstage for "Mr. Cellophane"
strike cap. Add
black clown coat
clown hat
white gloves
celluloid collar with tie attached

Change: after "Mr. Cellophane" into same as after "Funny
    Honey," but add
tie
sports jacket

Change: after Scene 6
strike jacket, tie. Add

cardigan
cap

Change: before last entrance
strike cardigan. Add
tie
jacket
cap

MARY MCCARTY AS MATRON

Act One—
wig
long, grey buttoned cotton gown (with badges)
black belt (with keys)
black hose
black heeled oxfords
white fur stole
green chiffon handkerchief

Change: before "When You're Good To Mama"
strike fur stole

Change: after "When You're Good To Mama"
strike handkerchief
Costume remains the same throughout the remainder of the
show

MICHAEL O'HAUGHEY AS MARY SUNSHINE

Act One—
wig
undergarment
stockings
salmon skirt
lace blouse
salmon lace jacket
high-heel beige shoes
fox fur
beige hat
beige gloves
pearls matching earrings

Change: after "We Both Reached For The Gun"
strike fur

Act Two—
  patterned green satin dress
  silk scarf
  beige hat
  beige gloves
  pearls, matching earrings

  Change: before "Me And My Baby"
  add fur

  Change: after "Me And My Baby"
  strike undergarment. Add
  men's boxer shorts
  break-away green dress
  fur
  hat

  Change: onstage at end of Scene 9
  stripped of wig, hat, dress

  Change: after Scene 9 makes change for "Bow"
  salmon skirt and jacket outfit

MICHON PEACOCK AS ANNIE

Act One—
  wig
  basic costume:
    flesh-colored tights; G string; black, silver, and red-
    striped torso; black stocking on R. leg; striped on L. leg;
    red shoe on L. foot; black and beige shoe with black bow
    on R. foot.
  black net shoulder cape with fur
  silver head band with feathers

  Change: for "Cell Block Tango"
  basic
  black plastic-striped net jail robe

  Change: for "Billy"
  bikini pants and bra over flesh tights
  silver shoes

red garter
black top hat

Change: "We Both Reached For The Gun"—Reporter
basic
grey tie
grey vest
grey fedora

Change: for "Roxie"
same as "Gun." Add
grey derby
grey gloves

Change: for Scene 13—Reporter
same as "Gun"

Act Two—
opening same as end of Act One

Change: for Scene 3
basic
jail robe
wig with a solid base

Change: for "Razzle Dazzle"
basic
ballerina black net short tutu with orange sequins
black velvet neck band
orange head dress with feathers

Change: Scene 9, Billy's exit and "Bows"
same as for "Billy" in Act One

CHERYL CLARK AS LIZ

Act One—
wig
basic costume:
    patterned tights; G string; black, silver, and red-striped
    torso; short beige skirt; grey hat; black shoes

Change: for "Cell Block Tango"
basic
black plastic-striped net jail robe

Change: for "Billy"
bikini pants and bra
silver shoes
black stockings
feather hat
flesh tights
red garter

Change: "We Both Reached For The Gun"—Reporter
basic
grey tie
grey vest
grey fedora
black shoes

Change: for "Roxie"
same as "Gun." Add
grey derby
grey gloves

Change: for Scene 12
black night slip

Act Two—
opening same as "Gun"—Reporter

Change: for "Razzle Dazzle"
basic
feathered hat
Maribou around hips
black shoes

Change: Scene 9, Billy's exit and "Bows"
same as for "Billy" in Act One

PAMELA SOUSA AS MONA

Act One—
wig

basic costume:
    beige tights; G string; black, silver and red-striped torso;
    black stockings; silver L. shoe; red R. shoe; garter belt;
    black L. garter; red R. garter
black boa
black feathered head band

Change: for "Cell Block Tango"
basic
black plastic-striped net jail robe

Change: for "Billy"
bikini pants and bra over flesh tights
silver shoes
black stockings
red garter

Change: for Scene 5—Mona
basic
jail robe
black shoes

Change: "We Both Reached For The Gun"—Reporter
basic
garter belt
right black stocking
red and silver shoes
grey vest
tie
grey fedora

Change: for "Roxie"
same as "Gun." Add
grey derby
grey gloves

Change: for Scene 12
black night slip

Act Two—
    opening same as "Gun"—Reporter

CANDY BROWN AS JUNE

Act One—
  wig
  basic costume:
    leotard with left bosom covered with elastic flesh mesh
    and sequin butterfly, waist section silver lame, finishing
    in red and black satin; flesh-colored panty hose, red and
    black striped stocking on R. leg; black stocking on L. leg;
    garters; black T-strap shoe on L. foot; silver T-strap shoe
    on R. leg
  gold cloche hat
  black satin beaded bow

  Change: for "Cell Block Tango"
  basic
  black plastic-striped net jail robe

  Change: for "Billy"
  pink and purple bikini and bra over flesh tights
  gold "boater" hat
  silver garter
  red garter

  Change: for "We Both Reached For The Gun"
  basic
  green tie
  black and red checked vest
  tan fedora

  Change: for "Roxie"
  same as "Gun." Add
  grey derby
  grey gloves

  Change: for Scene 13—Reporter
  same as "Gun"

Act Two—
  opening same as "Gun"—Reporter

Change: for Scene **3**
basic
jail robe

Change: End of Scene 1—Assistant to dress "Mr. Cellophane"
basic

Change: for "Razzle Dazzle"
basic
red boa
sequined bowler hat
pasties

Change: beginning of Scene 9—Reporter
same as "We Both Reached For The Gun"

Change: Scene 9, Billy's exit
same as for "Billy" in Act One

Change: for "Bows"
basic
black boa
black head band

Change: for "Razzle Dazzle"
basic
sequin top hat
handless gloves—rose-colored
silver lame neck bow
silver spat on L. foot

Change: Scene 9, Billy's exit
same as for "Billy" in Act One

Change: for "Bows"
basic
sequin bow (optional)
cloche hat (optional)

Charlene Ryan as Go-To-Hell Kitty

wig
basic costume:
  beige tights, G string; black, silver, and red striped torso; black stocking with red and white striped sock on L. leg; red stocking on R. leg; red T-strap shoe on R. foot; silver T-strap shoe on L. foot
string skirt
black fur muff
hat

Change: for "Billy"
bikini pants and bra over flesh tights
silver shoes
black stocking on L. leg
red garter
gold "boater" hat
*own hair

Change: for "We Both Reached For The Gun"
basic
orange tie
beige vest
beige fedora

Change: for "Roxie"
same as "Gun." Add
grey derby
grey gloves

Change: Scene 12—Go-To-Hell Kitty
beige tights
pink pajamas with tie
blue fur-trimmed coat
*own hair down and curly

Change: during Scene 12
strikes coat

Change: after Scene 12 for Scene 13. Adds
strait-jacket

Act Two—
> *Change:* for Scene 3
> basic, without knee sock
> red Chinese robe
> *own hair

> *Change:* for "Razzle Dazzle"
> basic
> yellow clown's collar
> butterfly wings
> flowered derby

> *Change:* after Scene 6 for Scene 8—Justice
> beige tights
> silver sandals
> mirrored G string
> bra
> white net overdress
> red and white stripe hat

> *Change:* for "Bows"
> basic
> black fur muff

GRACIELE DANIELE AS HUNYAK

Act One—
> basic costume:
>> silver fabric torso with black and red stripes; skirting around bottom; red and black stocking for L. leg; black kneesock with red cuff R. leg; beige tights black shoe L. foot; red shoe R. foot
> velvet and rhinestone cloche hat

> *Change:* for "Cell Block Tango"
> Hunyak wig
> basic
> black plastic-striped net jail robe

> *Change:* for Scene 5 and for "Billy"
> bikini and bra over flesh tights

silver shoes
black stocking L. leg
red garter
jail robe over

Change: to go into "Billy"
strike jail robe and Hunyak wig. Add
gold "boater" hat

Change: "We Both Reached For The Gun"—Reporter
basic
beige tie
checked vest
grey hat

Change: for "Roxie"
same as "Gun." Add
grey derby
grey gloves

Change: for Scene 13—Reporter
same as "Gun"

Act Two—
opening same as "Gun"—Reporter

Change: for Scene 4—Hunyak
gold sequin leotard
beige tights
blue and pink housedress over
beige ballet slippers
Hunyak wig

Change: onstage, end of Scene 4
strike housedress

Change: for "Razzle Dazzle"
basic
red cape
black ruffle at neck
black top hat

pink glove L. hand
pink flower at crotch

Change: for Scene 9, Billy's exit
same as for "Billy" in Act One

Change: for "Bows"
gold leotard
silver shoes
Hunyak wig

GENE FOOTE AS AARON

Act One—
basic costume
black leotard with cutouts on sides
tights—one pink leg, one grey with black opera stocking
black shoes, silver heels
white dickie
white gloves
black top hat
cane

Change: during "Cell Block Tango" for "Tap Dance"
black leotard
Black character shoes
tux dickie
tuxedo
bowler hat
cane

Change: before "Tap Dance"
strike cane

Change: before "We Both Reached For The Gun"—Reporter
black leotard
grey spats
striped tie
black striped vest
grey hat

Change: before "Roxie"
black leotard
tuxedo dickie
grey bowler hat
grey gloves

Change: after "Roxie," for Scene 13—Reporter
black leotard
grey spats
striped tie
black striped vest
grey hat

Act Two—
Opening same as end of Act One

Change: for "Velma Takes The Stand"
brown striped shirt
full tuxedo
red tie
straw boater

Change: after "Velma Takes The Stand" for Scene 4
brown striped shirt
brown pants
brown and white shoes
maroon tie
carry brown jacket

Change: after Scene 4 for "Razzle Dazzle"
black leotard
G string
pasties
top hat with feathers
black shoes with silver heels

Change: after "Razzle Dazzle" for Scene 9
same as for "We Both Reached For The Gun"

Change: for "The Act" skirt change with **Ann Reinking**
black leotard

black tux coat
white dickie
straw boater

Change: for "Bow"
basic outfit with
white gloves
top hat
cane

CHRISTOPHER CHADMAN AS FRED CASELY

Act One—
black tuxedo
white shirt
bow tie
black socks
black shoes
black fedora

Change: after "All That Jazz" for "Tap Dance"
basic costume:
black leotard with grey and silver stripes, orange sleeves
red stripe on R. leg
black shoes
black tuxedo over leotard
black derby

Change: for "We Both Reached For The Gun"—Reporter
black leotard
checked vest
tie
fedora

Change: for "Roxie"
black tuxedo over leotard
grey spats
grey gloves

Change: for end of Scene 13—Reporter
black leotard
checked vest

tie
fedora

Act Two—
same as end of Scene 13

Change: for "Velma Takes The Stand"
black tuxedo
straw boater

Change: for end of Scene 4
black leotard

Change: for "Razzle Dazzle"
leotard
blue vest
derby

Change: end of "Razzle Dazzle"—Fred Casely
tuxedo outfit

Change: for "Bow"
leotard
black hat

RICHARD KORTHAZE AS SERGEANT FOGARTY
Act One—
leotard, striped top, orange trunks, black R. leg, grey L. leg,
    black shoes
black and white vest
red print tie
straw boater

Change: for "Funny Honey"—Policeman
police uniform (leotard underneath)
police hat

Change: for "Tap Dance"
black tuxedo

dickie
straw boater
black shoes

Change: for Scene 8—Tailor
morning suit
dickie, tie

Change: for "We Both Reached For The Gun"—Reporter
leotard outfit
grey plaid vest
tie
black fedora
black shoes

Change: for "Roxie"
leotard outfit
dickie
grey spats
gloves
grey bowler hat

Change: after "Roxie" for Scene 13—Reporter
leotard
grey plaid vest
tie
black fedora

Act Two—
opening same as end of Act One

Change: for "Razzle Dazzle"
leotard
white clown collar with tie
red and white striped gloves
bald pate

Change: after "Razzle Dazzle" for Scene 9
leotard
disguises of the jury

Change: for "Bows"
leotard
old man's disguise from jury

Paul Solen as Bailiff

Act One—
  basic costume:
    white jersey, striped with black; black trunks; suspenders;
    grey stocking L. leg; red stocking R. leg; red shoes; cap
  bow tie

  Change: for "Tap Dance"
  tuxedo over "basic"
  black shoes

  Change: for "We Both Reached For The Gun"—Reporter
  basic
  red plaid vest
  tie

  Change: for "Roxie"
  basic
  dickie
  black bowler
  grey gloves
  black shoes
  grey spats

  Change: after "Roxie" for Scene 13—Reporter
  basic
  red plaid vest
  tie

Act Two—
  for "Strut"
  black tights
  white shirt
  tie
  black jacket
  black shoes
  grey spats

grey gloves
black bowler

Change: for Scene 3—Master of Ceremonies and "Velma
    Takes The Stand"
basic
tuxedo outfit
straw boater

Change: for Scene 4—Bailiff
police uniform

Change: for "Razzle Dazzle"
basic
collar
head band with fringe

Change: for Scene 9—Reporter
basic
red plaid vest
tie

Change: for Scene 9—"The Act"—Page
basic
red jacket
red pillbox hat

Change: for "Bows"
same as opening of Act One

GARY GENDELL AS COURT CLERK

Act One—
    basic costume:
        black jersey; red and grey striped tank top; grey and
        black trunks; black stocking L. leg; grey stocking R. leg;
        red shoes
    hat
    one white glove

Change: for Scene 2—Policeman
police uniform

Change: for Scene 4 and 7—Master of Ceremonies
tuxedo outfit
straw boater

Change: for "We Both Reached For The Gun" and Scene
12—Reporter
basic
red shoes
grey gloves
grey spats
dickie
grey bowler

Act Two—
for "Me And My Baby"
black tights
tuxedo jacket
white dickie
black bow tie
grey hat
grey spats
white gloves
black shoes

Change: for "Razzle Dazzle"
basic
red shoes
big pink and white polka dot bow tie
black and white spangled, sequin vest
straw boater
cane

Change: for Scene 9—Court Clerk
basic
tights
police jacket

Change: for Scene 8—Uncle Sam
Uncle Sam cape and hat: red, white, blue with stars

Change: for "Bows"
basic
sequin vest
white gloves

PAUL SOLEN AS HARRY

Act One—
  basic costume:
    beige net jersey, black stripes; beige trunks; red stocking
    L. leg; tan stocking R. leg; black and white shoes; sock
    on R. foot
  grey fedora
  tie

  Change: for Scene 2—Policeman
  police uniform

  Change: for "Tap Dance"
  tuxedo outfit
  black bowler

  Change: for "We Both Reached For The Gun"—Reporter
  basic
  grey vest
  grey fedora
  tie

  Change: for "Roxie"
  basic
  black tuxedo
  dickie with bow tie
  grey bowler
  grey gloves
  grey spats

  Change: for Scene 12—Harry
  suit of white under (boxer shorts)

Act Two—
  basic

lab coat
striped pants

Change: for "Velma Takes The Stand"
tuxedo outfit
straw boater

Change: for Scene 4—Holds scaffold ladder for Hunyak
basic
neck ruff
mylar chest disc
white bowler with plume
mylar cheek patches

Change: for "Razzle Dazzle"
add: white bowler

Change: for Scene 6—The Judge
robe
mask
fool's folly

Change: for Scene 9—Page
basic
red jacket
red pillbox hat

Change: for "Bows"
add: neck ruff

MICHAEL VITA AS MARTIN HARRISON

Act One—
  basic costume:
    red jersey with black and silver stripe; beige trunks; black
    tights with red stripes; jewelled belt; red and black shoes
  top hat
  cane
  black scarf
  black sock and garter

Change: for "They Both Reached For The Gun" and Scene
    13—Reporter
basic
grey vest
black tie
brown hat

Act Two—
opening same as end of Act One

Change: for Scene 6—Martin Harrison
basic
tan suit
tan shirt
tie
brown shoes
brown socks

Change: for "Bows"
basic
brown hat

PROPERTY LIST

Furniture Props
piano
piano stool
jail bars unit
medium size table
door frame and door

Hand Props
flask
3 electric jail bars
paper money
6 plume fans
black chair (doubles)
newspaper ("Roxie Rocks Chicago")
trick milk glass
plate with food
a fork and knife
stack of fan mail
stack of newspapers
bouquet of flowers
round table microphone
bouquet of red roses
pad and pencils
2 megaphones
4 tambourines
cigars
cigarettes
1 legal document
briefcase (Billy)
scale and sword (Miss Justice)
cardboard bed cut-out
whistle (police type)
microphone on stand

BASEMENT

Furniture Props
Roxie's bed and headboard
large table (doubles)
4 chairs (double)
Billy's desk
2 office chairs
silent valet
standing mirror
Kitty's bed and headboard
table and bench (doubles)

Hand Props
pistol
bed sheet
clipboard and pen
butt can
tin cup
cardboard box with assorted liquor bottles
deck of cards
4 legal statements
telephone
boutonniere with vase (Billy)
tailor's pants (Billy)
tailor's pin cushion with pins
tailor's tape measure
tailor's chalk
2 prop hands with rings on finger
newspaper (Chicago)
desk blotter
ash tray and cigarette lighter
2 ink wells
shoe box with shoes (rhinestone buckles)
paper money
2 ash trays
2 boxes of matches
cigarettes
cigar

Personal Props
rosary beads (Roxie)

robe (Roxie)
knitting with needles (Matron)
flask (Velma)
wallet (Casely)

STAGE LEFT

Furniture Props
cell bar unit (doubles)
stool (doubles)
small table
2 chairs (doubles)
12 stool jury box

Hand Props
newspaper (dressing)
2 newspapers ("Crime of the Year" and "Feindish Double
    Homicide")
3 electrical jail bars
cigarettes
sculpture and clay
visitor's screen
cigars
flask
1 newspaper ("Roxie Rocks Chicago")
stretcher
6 plume fans
pads and pencils
machine gun
2 flash cameras
coat tree
witness stand
2 megaphones
pistol
blackboard with diagram
wheelchair
3 tambourines
Hunyak dummy
American flag on a pole
Bible
radio
bouquet of red roses

Personal Props
ring, scarf, and fur (Matron)
money (Velma)
money (Matron)
cane (Company)
strait-jacket (Kitty)
juggler's balls (Billy)
stick with balloon

jury box props:
toupee and mustache
gray beard
5 asstd. pairs of glasses
mittens
fake nose mask
fake nose and cheek mask
flask
large bow tie and collar
3 different style mustaches
hearing horn
white cane

Technical

1. black moustache
   toupee
   ladies hat
   lourgnette
2. nose (turned up)
   Pince Nez
3. glasses with nose
4. blind man glasses
   cane (on floor)
5. round rim glasses
   big red nose
   fake fat cheeks
6. none
7. rectangle glasses
   grey beard
   hearing aid under seat on floor
8. whiskey flask

FRONT – ON STAGE

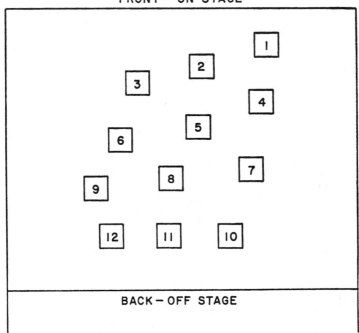

BACK – OFF STAGE

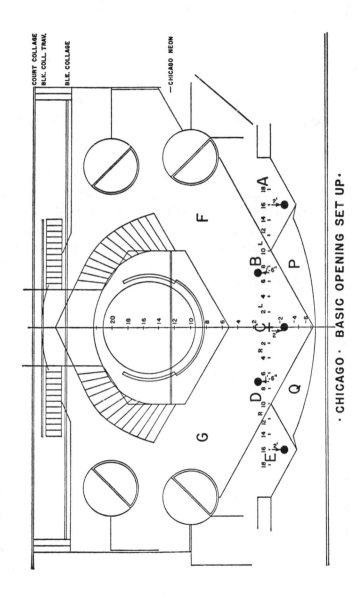

· CHICAGO · BASIC OPENING SET UP ·

123

NO SEX PLEASE, WE'RE BRITISH
Anthony Marriott and Alistair Foot

Farce / 7 m., 3 f. / Int.

A young bride who lives above a bank with her husband who is the assistant manager, innocently sends a mail order off for some Scandinavian glassware. What comes is Scandinavian pornography. The plot revolves around what is to be done with the veritable floods of pornography, photographs, books, films and eventually girls that threaten to engulf this happy couple. The matter is considerably complicated by the man's mother, his boss, a visiting bank inspector, a police superintendent and a muddled friend who does everything wrong in his reluctant efforts to set everything right, all of which works up to a hilarious ending of closed or slamming doors. This farce ran in London over eight years and also delighted Broadway audiences.

"Titillating and topical."
- "NBC TV"

"A really funny Broadway show."
- "ABC TV"

ALSO AVAILABLE FROM SAMUEL FRENCH

PETER PAN
A musical based on the play by James M. Barrie

Music by Mark Charlap and Jule Styne
Lyrics by Carolyn Leigh, Betty Comden and Adolph Green

Musical Fantasy / 28 characters w/doubling / 4 ext., 2 int.
First produced on Broadway with Mary Martin and Cyril Richard and more recently a major hit starring Cathy Rigby, this is one of the world's most celebrated musicals. Here is all the charm of J.M. Barrie's Peter Pan, Tinker Bell, the children Wendy, Michael and John, pirates and Indians, embellished with show-stopping songs, "Never Never Land", "I Won't Grow Up" and "I'm Flying".

"As wondrous as it has been since in first appeared on Broadway."
— *Boston Globe*

"Bountiful, good-natured. ... A vastly amusing show."
— *N.Y. Times*

"A delightful entertainment. . . . The young in heart of all ages will love it."
— *N. Y. Daily Mirror*

"The musical version of this most endearing of all theatrical fantasies is a captivating show."
— *N.Y. Daily News*

SECRET GARDEN
The Musical

Book and Lyrics by Marsha Norman
Music by Lucy Simon
Based on the novel by Frances Hodgson Burnett

12m, 10f, 1f child, (doubling possible) / Ints., exts.

This enchanting classic of children's literature is now a brilliant musical by a Pulitzer Prize winning playwright. Orphaned in India, an 11 year old girl returns to Yorkshire to live with an embittered, reclusive uncle and his invalid son. The estate includes a magic locked garden. Flashbacks, dream sequences, a strolling chorus of ghosts, and some of the most beautiful music ever written for Broadway dramatize *The Secret Garden*'s compelling tale of regeneration. This Tony Award winner is a treasure for children and adults.

"Elegant, entrancing.... The best American musical of the Broadway season."
– Time

"A splendid, intelligent musical...It's all you can hope for in children's theatre. But the best surprise is that this show is the most adult new musical of the season."
– U.S.A. Today

"Revels in theatrical imagination [and] achieves the irresistible appeal that moves audiences to standing ovations."
– Christian Science Monitor

SAMUELFRENCH.COM

ANNE & GILBERT
Music by Bob Johnston and Nancy White
Book by Jeff Hochhauser
Lyrics by Nancy White, Bob Johnston and Jeff Hochhauser

Based on the novels *Anne of Avonlea* and *Anne of the Island*
by L.M. Montgomery

All Groups / Musical / 8m, 6f, many extras
Based on the sequel novels to Anne of Green Gables, this new
Canadian musical continues the story of Anne Shirley's life. Set in
the village of Avonlea and at Redmond College in Halifax, Anne
and Gilbert follows Anne's journey to young adulthood and her
romance with high school academic rival, Gilbert Blythe. Gilbert
is in love with Anne, but she seems to be immune to his declara-
tions of love. In the end, Anne realizes what everyone else already
knows: that Gilbert is the love of her life.

"Anne and Gilbert is a marvel."
- *The Toronto Star*

"When the curtain fell, I was disappointed to see it all end."
- *Variety*

"Anne and Gilbert [is a] treasure of a show. A timeless and eloquent
love story filled with charming characters and beautiful music."
- *Lennie Macpherson, Guardian*